**East Midlands**
Edited by Justine Horne

First published in Great Britain in 2008 by:
Young Writers
Remus House
Coltsfoot Drive
Peterborough
PE2 9JX
Telephone: 01733 890066
Website: www.youngwriters.co.uk

All Rights Reserved

© Copyright Contributors 2008

SB ISBN 978-1 84431 752 3

# Foreword

Young Writers' Big Green Poetry Machine is a showcase for our nation's most brilliant young poets to share their thoughts, hopes and fears for the planet they call home.

Young Writers was established in 1991 to nurture creativity in our children and young adults, to give them an interest in poetry and an outlet to express themselves. Seeing their work in print will encourage them to keep writing as they grow, and become our poets of tomorrow.

Selecting the poems has been challenging and immensely rewarding. The effort and imagination invested by these young writers makes their poems a pleasure to enjoy reading time and time again.

# Contents

**Annie Holgate Junior School, Hucknall**
| | |
|---|---|
| Jessica Richards (9) | 1 |
| Keillie-Ellen Scrimshaw (10) | 1 |
| Jordan Finney (11) | 2 |
| Louise Duvel (10) | 2 |
| Alex Hannigan (11) | 3 |
| Frankie Whitehouse (11) | 3 |
| Brandon Wynn (11) | 4 |
| Autumn Spencer (10) | 4 |
| Courtney Evans (11) | 5 |
| Thomas Wigginton (11) | 5 |
| Jade Horton (10) | 6 |
| James Lobb (10) | 6 |

**Besthorpe Primary School, Newark**
| | |
|---|---|
| Verity Custance (9) | 6 |
| Lizzie Wood (9) | 7 |

**Bracken Leas School, Brackley**
| | |
|---|---|
| Alexander Yearsley (8) | 7 |
| Eleanor Coleman (8) | 8 |
| Thomas Beckett (8) | 9 |
| Rachel Toland (8) | 10 |
| Caitlin Morrison (8) | 11 |
| Lauren Ruff (8) | 12 |
| Hayley Ashley (8) | 13 |
| Lucy Jeffery (8) | 14 |

**Church Drive Primary School, Arnold**
| | |
|---|---|
| Danni Beardall (10) | 14 |
| Jake Robinson (9) | 15 |
| Michael van der Sanden (10) | 15 |
| Jake Smithard (10) | 16 |
| Katie Stilwell (9) | 16 |
| Chloe Williams (10) | 17 |
| Joshua Curtis (9) | 17 |
| Polly-Anne Rastall (10) | 18 |
| Sarah Cassady (9) | 18 |

| | |
|---|---|
| Kiran Kaur  (10) | 19 |
| Molly Warrener-Batchelor  (10) | 19 |
| Brynn Morris  (9) | 20 |
| Shaan Kaur  (10) | 21 |
| Millie Richardson  (10) | 21 |
| Olivia Bragg  (9) | 22 |
| Georgia Kingham  (10) | 22 |
| Alicia Belshaw  (9) | 23 |
| Connor Skinner  (9) | 23 |
| Holly Wardle  (10) | 24 |
| Dylan Sutcliffe  (10) | 24 |
| Laura Hopewell  (10) | 25 |
| Alice Clarke  (10) | 25 |

**East Markham Primary School, East Markham**

| | |
|---|---|
| Amy Evans  (8) | 26 |
| Katie Whelan  (10) | 26 |
| Isaac Higgs  (9) | 27 |
| George Thorne  (10) | 28 |
| Daniel Gagg  (11) | 28 |
| Derek Milton  (10) | 29 |
| Lucy Garnett  (9) | 29 |
| Alexander Ridgway  (9) | 30 |
| Kyle Smith  (11) | 30 |
| Lauren Gardiner  (11) | 31 |
| Amy-Sue Johnson  (9) | 31 |
| Lauren Norman  (11) | 32 |
| Sarah Eakin  (9) | 33 |
| Megan Eakin  (11) | 34 |
| Lewis Foley  (10) | 35 |
| George Shaw  (10) | 36 |
| Ellie Clarson  (8) | 36 |
| Jack Higgs  (11) | 37 |
| Sophie Finch  (8) | 37 |
| Emily Holmes  (9) | 38 |
| Laura Beckett  (10) | 39 |
| Emily Davies  (10) | 40 |
| Jake Casburn  (11) | 41 |
| Matthew Steels  (11) | 42 |
| Danielle Cosgrove  (10) | 42 |

### Fairmeadows Foundation Primary School, Newhall

| | |
|---|---|
| Bethany Ashmore (7) | 43 |
| Tamzin Irvine-Brentnall (8) | 43 |
| Joshua Smith (8) | 43 |
| Kayleigh Ison (8) | 44 |
| Elly-Mae Griffiths (8) | 44 |
| Kiara Knight (8) | 44 |
| Kaytlin Dyche (8) | 45 |
| Caitlin Rees (8) | 45 |
| Brandon Hook (8) | 45 |
| India Oakey (7) | 46 |
| Reece Clamp (8) | 46 |
| Amber Ottaway (8) | 46 |
| Joseph Hyde (7) | 46 |
| Zak Morris (7) | 47 |
| Kane Clamp (7) | 47 |
| Luke Wadsworth (8) | 47 |
| Mollie Moon (7) | 47 |
| Sophie McMahon (7) | 48 |

### Heymann Primary School, West Bridgford

| | |
|---|---|
| Emma Sunderland (10) | 48 |
| Hania Hickling (10) | 49 |
| Daniel Hardy (11) | 49 |
| Matthew Quayle (11) | 50 |
| Joshua Lee (11) | 50 |
| Lydia Williams (11) | 51 |
| Owais Hussain (10) | 51 |
| Sophie Turner (11) | 52 |
| Jaskaran Kaur (11) | 52 |
| Catriona Higgins (11) | 53 |
| Didi Sadeq (11) | 53 |
| Tom Polkinghorne (11) | 54 |
| Stephanie Dewan (11) | 54 |
| Rhia Moore (11) | 55 |
| Michael Butcher (11) | 55 |
| Gurpreet Sehmbi (11) | 56 |
| Hannah Shepheard (11) | 57 |
| Azeem Razak (11) | 58 |
| Mark Webster (11) | 58 |
| Pavandeep Lakhanpal (11) | 59 |

Michael Lamb  (11)   59
Victoria Tantum  (11)   60
Oli Kitt  (11)   60
Hassiba Boukari  (11)   61
Alana Lowe  (10)   61
Lulu Song  (11)   62

## Holly Hill Primary School, Selston
Zoe Tissington  (11)   62
Eleanor Sewell  (11)   63
Ross Whyatt  (10)   63
Georgia Culligan  (11)   64
Katie Moss  (11)   64
Mia Maciejewski  (11)   65
Beth Moss  (11)   65
Jade Fantom  (11)   66
Nathan Dudley  (11)   66
Clara Gray  (11)   67
Danielle Stevenson  (11)   67
Emma Trower  (10)   68
Brady Tagg  (10)   69

## Kingswood Primary School, Corby
Jessica Davidson  (10)   69
Georgia Hargin  (9)   70
George Blackie  (9)   70
Anita Ullah  (10)   70
Robyn Smith  (9)   71
Samantha Matthews  (11)   71
Kelseylea Burgess  (9)   71
Sai Stephenson  (11)   72
James Ingram  (11)   72
Abigail Storrie  (10)   73
Courtney Cook  (10)   73
Christopher Hart  (11)   74
Kieran McNairn  (9)   74
Craig Doctor  (11)   74
Joshua Jarman  (11)   75
Dante Sharples  (9)   75
Dominic Devlin  (11)   75

| | |
|---|---|
| Damla Akgul  (10) | 76 |
| Lauren Stedman  (10) | 76 |

## Linden Primary School, Evington
| | |
|---|---|
| Safanah Riaz  (11) | 77 |
| Gurdit Singh Dosanjh  (10) | 77 |
| Ndumiso Nyoni  (10) | 78 |
| Molly Furnival-Phillips  (11) | 78 |
| Jaisel Odedra  (11) | 78 |
| Zainab Ahmad  (11) | 79 |
| Nasreen Bhana  (10) | 79 |
| Karan Chundavadara  (11) | 79 |
| Eleanor Forté  (11) | 80 |
| Vishnu Godhania  (11) | 80 |

## North Leverton Primary School, North Leverton
| | |
|---|---|
| Ella Mowbray, Owen Gamble & Daisy Marsh  (9) | 80 |
| Katrina Hayes  (10) | 81 |
| Bethany Bartram  (10) | 81 |

## Robert Miles Junior School, Bingham
| | |
|---|---|
| Ryan Wilcock  (11) | 82 |
| Dexter Turnbull  (11) | 82 |
| Dale Thomas  (11) | 83 |
| Lewis Cheung  (11) | 83 |
| Eleanor Cooke  (10) | 84 |
| Megan Wills  (11) | 86 |
| Stefan Rose  (11) | 87 |
| Grace Watts  (10) | 88 |
| Ellie Clark  (11) | 89 |
| Elizabeth Ryder  (11) | 90 |
| Matthew Coughtrey  (11) | 91 |

## Robin Hood Primary School, Mansfield
| | |
|---|---|
| Sineh McFarlane  (8) | 92 |
| Alex Morey  (8) | 92 |
| Owen Ives  (8) | 93 |
| Ryan Southall  (8) | 93 |
| Savannah Southway  (8) | 94 |
| Ryan Caudwell  (8) | 94 |

| | |
|---|---|
| Corey Roberts (8) | 95 |
| Luke West (9) | 95 |

## Rockingham Primary School, Corby
| | |
|---|---|
| Sam James-Molloy & Henry (11) | 95 |
| Meghan Hill (10) | 96 |
| Sad Maudarbux (11) | 97 |

## Ruskin Junior School, Wellingborough
| | |
|---|---|
| Latasha Fitzpatrick (11) | 97 |
| Tiffany Wallace (11) | 98 |
| Hanna Baldwin (11) | 98 |
| Stefan Benn (10) | 99 |
| Richard Simmons (11) | 99 |
| Bradley Souster (11) | 100 |
| Billy Vidler (11) | 100 |
| Kieran Potticary (11) | 101 |
| Alfie Parr (11) | 101 |
| Montell Ashby (11) | 102 |
| Billy Jones (11) | 102 |
| Jason Holt (11) | 103 |
| Brandon Richards (10) | 103 |
| Alexa Brannan (11) | 104 |
| Kieran Reeve (10) | 104 |
| Cain Clarke (11) | 105 |
| Barrington Abel (10) | 105 |
| Daniel McCullagh (11) | 106 |
| Keeley Dargue (11) | 106 |
| John Rowlatt (11) | 107 |
| Scott Millen Poole (11) | 107 |
| Aaron Strong (11) | 107 |
| Ryan Betts (11) | 108 |

## St Mary's CE Primary School, Kettering
| | |
|---|---|
| Jodie Wallace (9) | 108 |
| Katrina Newlyn (9) | 108 |
| Grace Sensier (9) | 109 |
| Jemma Hughes (8) | 109 |
| Patricia Anne V Mallare (8) | 110 |
| Hannah Strickland (9) | 110 |
| Yasmin Boyall (9) | 111 |

| | |
|---|---|
| Jade Leeson  (9) | 111 |
| Lauson Kenyon  (9) | 112 |
| Alisha Taylor  (9) | 112 |
| Tabitha Catlin  (9) | 113 |
| Luca Benedickter  (9) | 113 |
| Jai Sharma  (9) | 114 |

**St Michael's CE Primary School, Lincoln**

| | |
|---|---|
| Beth Green  (8) | 114 |
| Joshua Berry  (9) | 115 |
| Ellie Redfern  (9) | 115 |
| Jack Whittam  (8) | 116 |
| Grace Warren | 116 |
| Ella Good  (8) | 117 |
| Sophie Hill  (8) | 117 |
| Miss Reid's Class | 118 |
| Jessica Thursby  (8) | 119 |
| Dominic Marshall  (8) | 120 |
| Victoria Aitken  (10) | 120 |
| Henry Hutchings  (11) | 121 |
| Nicholas Scott  (8) | 121 |
| Robert Westwood | 122 |
| Dominic Contessa  (11) | 122 |
| Jake Hill  (11) | 122 |
| Alexander Staniforth  (9) | 123 |
| Matthew Thompson  (10) | 123 |
| Ellie Gibbon  (10) | 124 |
| Elloise Long  (9) | 124 |
| Matthew Scott  (10) | 125 |
| Joseph Brundell  (9) | 125 |
| Megan Rowland  (9) | 126 |
| Emily Gatford  (9) | 126 |
| Phoebe Erm  (8) | 127 |
| Sam Perkins  (7) | 127 |
| Jessica Fenwick  (8) | 128 |
| Amy Hall  (8) | 128 |
| James McKirdy  (9) | 129 |
| Christopher Appleby  (10) | 129 |
| Eleanor Burrows  (10) | 130 |
| Liam Smalley | 130 |
| Louisa Moxhay-Baker  (10) | 131 |

| | |
|---|---|
| Lauren Westwood | 131 |
| Tim Williams  (8) | 132 |
| William Lupton  (8) | 132 |
| Rebecca Clark  (9) | 132 |

**St Swithun's CE Primary School, Retford**

| | |
|---|---|
| Saffiah Sanders-Bailey  (9) | 133 |
| Emily Sly  (10) | 133 |
| Kai Denovan  (10) | 133 |
| Jade Swan  (10) | 134 |
| Jemma Creasy-Woodward  (10) | 134 |
| Ashley Mattingley  (10) | 135 |
| Yumi Li Vi  (9) | 135 |

**Sneinton CE Primary School, Sneinton**

| | |
|---|---|
| Sophie Pearce  (9) | 135 |
| Owen Newton  (9) | 136 |
| Leah Collingham  (8) | 136 |
| Jade Clarke  (9) | 137 |
| Lavantie Cameron  (9) | 137 |
| Ali Naseer  (8) | 137 |
| Ben Flavill  (9) | 138 |
| Billie Rose  (8) | 138 |

# The Poems

## Eco World

The Earth is like a rubbish dump
If we stopped littering it would be a lovely place
People would come to see our world
Maybe even from space.

The Earth is like a flashing sign
It flashes from colour to grey
If nobody does anything about it
Animals won't be able to stay.

The Earth is like a crystal
All pretty and beautiful
If we don't care about it
It will go dull.

The Earth is like a helpless child
Cradled in our hands
If only we stop polluting it
And leave it how it stands.

**Jessica Richards (9)**
**Annie Holgate Junior School, Hucknall**


## The Environment

The Earth is like a helpless child,
Cradled in our hands,
Everywhere you turn,
There is litter on the lands.

With the pollution and the gases in the air,
Our land will be a pollutant scare.

**Keillie-Ellen Scrimshaw (10)**
**Annie Holgate Junior School, Hucknall**

## The Terrible War

The terrible screams
Of the friends of the dead,
The good times they had
Stay in their heads.

Six months of training,
The machine gun fire,
The pile of the dead,
Gets higher and higher.

Why, oh why
Did it ever start?
What stops when you're shot
Is the beat of your heart.

The loving families,
Cry all of the night,
Nothing can bring them back,
Not even the strongest might.

**Jordan Finney (11)**
**Annie Holgate Junior School, Hucknall**


## Litter - Haikus

Litter's disgusting,
It's really, really smelly,
And it attracts rats.

You will see more rats,
Which can carry diseases,
That make people sick.

The smell is awful,
It is polluting the air,
By being around.

**Louise Duvel (10)**
**Annie Holgate Junior School, Hucknall**

## Litter

Litter, litter is really bad,
It makes people very sad.
Pick it up, please,
Or maybe you'll get a disease.

If we continue,
Rats will come,
Rats will patrol the streets,
Please pick up some.

**Alex Hannigan (11)**
**Annie Holgate Junior School, Hucknall**


## Litter,

Litter, litter,
You are bad.

Litter, litter,
You make people sad.

Litter, litter,
You bring rats.

Litter, litter,
You sometimes bring cats.

Litter, litter,
You really smell.

Litter, litter,
I will repel.

**Frankie Whitehouse (11)**
**Annie Holgate Junior School, Hucknall**

## War

War is very bad
It is so, so sad
You can die
But can't fly
You shoot a lot
Practising every shot
You catch a lot of men
And end up killing them.

**Brandon Wynn (11)**
**Annie Holgate Junior School, Hucknall**

## Litter,

Litter, litter,
Put it in bins,
Litter, litter,
Paper, cans, even tins.

Litter, litter,
Put it away,
Litter, litter,
Do it every day.

Litter, litter,
Do not drop it,
Litter, litter,
It might smell a bit.

So now you know,
Don't drop litter,
It could be harmful,
To a little critter.

**Autumn Spencer (10)**
**Annie Holgate Junior School, Hucknall**

## Saving Animals

Animals are dying,
I'm nearly crying,
People are hunting them down.

Animals are becoming extinct,
If you don't stop,
I'll be sad,
Because I love animals.

Animals are getting hunted in rainforests,
If you stop we will have some animals left,
Stop hunting them down,
Or without a doubt, they will die.

**Courtney Evans (11)**
**Annie Holgate Junior School, Hucknall**


## Pollution

Pollution, pollution
It is smelly,
Pollution, pollution
It comes from a car's belly.

Pollution, pollution
It's bad for you,
Pollution, pollution
It hurts people.

Pollution, pollution
It can be smoke,
Pollution, pollution
It makes people choke.

**Thomas Wigginton (11)**
**Annie Holgate Junior School, Hucknall**

## Poem About The Environment

Pollution is ruining our land,
Smoke is choking the air,
Walls are covered in graffiti,
We need to show we care.
There are car fumes in the air,
If we don't start walking,
All the land will go spare.

**Jade Horton (10)**
Annie Holgate Junior School, Hucknall


## Environment

The Earth is like a helpless child,
Cradled in our hands,
Please recycle,
Because we're slowly destroying lands.

The Earth is like a dustbin,
Dirty and dusty,
Even the metal
Is going rusty.

**James Lobb (10)**
Annie Holgate Junior School, Hucknall


## Recycling

Put recycling in a recycling bin!
Plastic, cardboard, paper and tin.
Do not put litter on the floor,
Or the world will not be a nice place anymore!

**Verity Custance (9)**
Besthorpe Primary School, Newark

## Recycling

R emember our
E nvironment is
C ool if
Y ou try
C aring for
L ittle things
I f so
N ow try
G et recycling!

**Lizzie Wood (9)**
**Besthorpe Primary School, Newark**


## The Last Sounds Of The Rainforest
*(Inspired by 'The Sound Collector' by Roger McGough)*

Some strangers came last night
They were dressed all in grey
Put the forest sounds into a truck
And took them all away.

The whooshing of the waterfalls,
The cawing of the macaws,
The hissing of the sepia snakes,
The rustling of the pleasant plants,
The bellowing of the amusing apes,
The snoring of the gentle tribes,
The croaking of the poisonous frogs,
The silence of the black beetles.

Some loggers came last night,
They didn't leave a twig,
They left us in a rainforest graveyard,
Life will never be the same again.

**Alexander Yearsley (8)**
**Bracken Leas School, Brackley**

## The Sounds Of The Rainforest
*(Inspired by 'The Sound Collector' by Roger McGough)*

Some tall people came today
All dressed in black and grey
They put all the sounds into a tray
And took them all away.

They took the sounds of:
The water as white as snow
Rushing as fast as a racing car
Tribespeople talking, shouting, playing
Slithering snakes all slimy
The cawing of the multicoloured macaws
The rumbling of the leaping leopards
The sloths' claws scraping
The sound of pistachio leaves rustling
The rain going pitter-patter
The sound of the moody music playing in the village
The blowing of the trees
Loggers cutting down the trees
Tree stumps looking like graves
The singing of the beautiful birds
The swish-swashing of the grass
The tiptoeing of the hunters
Like mice.

Some loggers came today
I didn't know their names
They just left us in silence
Life will never be the same.

**Eleanor Coleman (8)**
**Bracken Leas School, Brackley**

## The Song Of The Lost Rainforest
*(Inspired by 'The Sound Collector' by Roger McGough)*

Some strangers came this evening,
Dressed in green and grey,
Placed the forest sounds into a truck
And drove them away.

The stamping of the colossal elephants,
The hiss, hiss of the snakes,
When water falls off the elephant leaves,
The dripping sound it makes,
The cawing of the multicoloured macaws,
The croaking of the poisonous frogs,
When the tribes pass,
All the vines they tore,
The call of a monkey,
The toss of the river,
The roar of a cheetah
And all the leaves that quiver,
The leap of a lazy leopard,
The animals creeping around,
The creaking call of the twigs,
When they're lying on the ground.

Some loggers came this evening,
They did not leave their names,
The graveyard silence
Left us all in shame.

**Thomas Beckett (8)**
**Bracken Leas School, Brackley**

## The Last Rainforest
*(Inspired by 'The Sound Collector' by Roger McGough)*

A stranger came this morning
Dressed only in green
Put the forest sounds into a truck
And never set them free.

The sounds of the animals creeping around
The rustling hazel leaves lying on the ground
The multicoloured macaws flying up above
The snakes hissing loudly
The plants swaying quickly
Tribal people taking tiny steps
Water running and roaring
Everyone heard it.

A logger came this morning
He didn't leave a thing
He left us only silence
However did it begin?

**Rachel Toland (8)**
**Bracken Leas School, Brackley**

## Torture In The Rainforest
*(Inspired by 'The Sound Collector' by Roger McGough)*

Some men came to our village today
They were dressed in yellow jackets
They cut down all the trees in their way
And the happiness went away with it.

The leaping of the leopards
The water swishing, swaying
And all the children playing
And chattering all day long
The croaking of the frogs
The cawing of the macaws
Lovely lime leaves as huge as elephant ears
The monkeys go *ooo-ooo*
The tribes go *boo*

Some loggers came to our village today
They didn't leave their names
They drove away silently
Leaving us in shame.

**Caitlin Morrison (8)**
**Bracken Leas School, Brackley**

## I Saw A Stranger Last Night
*(Inspired by 'The Sound Collector' by Roger McGough)*

I saw a stranger last night
All dressed in black
He put the forest's song into a truck
And drove it away.

The swishing and swirling of the avocado and lime leaves
Both the rippling and the streaming of the sapphire river
The grumbling and the yowling of the wild animals
The crawling and creeping of the Bak-aka tribe hunting for
                                                            their dinner
The crackling of the dead leaves on the forest floor
The croaking of the frogs near a gurgling creek.

The loggers came last night
They left no sound at all
Only silence
Life will never be the same.

**Lauren Ruff (8)**
**Bracken Leas School, Brackley**

## The Last Sounds
*(Inspired by 'The Sound Collector' by Roger McGough)*

Some men came this morning
Dressed all in green
Put all the sounds in a bag
And drove them away

Now, no slimy snakes are hissing
No birds are tweeting in the treetops
No tree frogs are resting on the tree stumps
No leaves are rattling on the ground
No bushes are shaking in the wind
No tribes are hunting for their meal
No macaws are cawing in the trees
No waterfalls are crashing on the rocks

Some loggers came this morning
They didn't leave their names
They only left the forest in silence
Now life will never be the same.

**Hayley Ashley (8)**
**Bracken Leas School, Brackley**

## The Greatly Lost Song Of The Rainforest
*(Inspired by 'The Sound Collector' by Roger McGough)*

Some strangers called at noon
All dressed in brown and grey
Put all the sounds into a truck
And drove them all away.

The cawing of a scarlet macaw
The hissing of a slithering, sly snake
When raindrops fall on the large lime leaves
The dripping sound it makes
The croak, croak of a frog
The big steps of a gorilla
The rumble of a lazy leopard
The call of a slow, sluggish sloth
The screeching of a mad monkey

Some loggers called at noon
They didn't leave their names
Left us only silence
Life won't be the same.

**Lucy Jeffery (8)**
**Bracken Leas School, Brackley**


## Your Choice

Waste is the colour black and dark red,
It feels like everyone is dying
And smells like lifeless, smelly fish.
It tastes like red-hot, burning chilli
And makes me feel saddened inside.

Recycling is the colour dark purple,
It feels like everyone saving lives
And smells like fresh green grass.
It tastes like warm honey
And makes me feel happy inside.

**Danni Beardall (10)**
**Church Drive Primary School, Arnold**

## Our Big World!

O n the world there are many beautiful things to look at
U gly world it will be if you keep polluting it
R ainforests are disappearing and animals are becoming extinct

B alloon: our world is a big one - you blow it up and one day it will pop!
I f the world bursts, we will burst too: you don't want that to happen, do you?
G oodness is a very valuable thing, so help it live, come on

W hen we save the world, everyone will be happy
O therwise everything will go wrong, it has already started
R un away from the horror the world has become? No!
L isten! Learn and change. If you save the world, the biggest prize will come. Life itself
D one? Not yet, you still have a lot of work to do, the world of forever gardeners.

**Jake Robinson (9)**
**Church Drive Primary School, Arnold**


## The Big World

S ave our world, it is
A beautiful world. Littering is like
V andalism to the
E arth.

E arth, our planet, is dying. The
A rctic is melting. The
R ainforests are wearing away
T he energy we use
H as an effect on the ozone layer. Stop, think and save!

**Michael van der Sanden (10)**
**Church Drive Primary School, Arnold**

## Help The World

Help! I am dying
Because no one puts their wrappers in the bin, or walks anywhere
And they don't even share a car to school.
They're even cutting down trees!
Soon it will be all roads: no grass, no trees, no rivers,
No animals, no people . . .
No world.

**Jake Smithard (10)**
**Church Drive Primary School, Arnold**


## Help The World

The Earth is like this now:

The Earth is misty grey,
It smells like a smoky fire,
It tastes like poison,
It makes me feel sad for the future
And it makes the Earth feel poorly.

But it could be like this if we help save the world:

The Earth is green and blue,
It smells like refreshing roses,
It tastes like soft, warm bread,
It makes me feel over the moon
And it makes the Earth feel better than ever.

**Katie Stilwell (9)**
**Church Drive Primary School, Arnold**

## Recycle Paper

R ecycle paper and any other things
E ven
C ans
Y ou need to save energy
C os the Earth needs us. The Earth is just a dead
L ittle sphere ready to
E xplode, so watch our

P lanet
A nd think before you even start to
P ollute our
E arth
*R ight!* Get a move on! Go!

**Chloe Williams (10)**
**Church Drive Primary School, Arnold**


## Big And Green

Recycling must be done
If you don't, animals will die.
Killing people is bad.
Don't burn houses and woods,
Don't put litter on the floor,
Or,
The world will die.
Our solar system will end.
Please stop now before it happens, OK?
Be big and green, not selfish and mean!

**Joshua Curtis (9)**
**Church Drive Primary School, Arnold**

## Have You Got A Heart?

People every day destroying our Earth,
Causing global warming,
Killing animals' homes,
Even slaughtering animals themselves.
You're even killing *your* life.

So how can you save the world?
Well you can . . .
Stop using your cars all the time,
Turn your lights off when you leave the house,
Put your litter in the bin.
Will you make a change?
Have you got a heart?

**Polly-Anne Rastall (10)**
Church Drive Primary School, Arnold

## The World

From my dirty window,
The world looks like smoky grey venom.
It smells like poisonous fuel.
It tastes like polluted air.
It makes me feel trapped in a deep hole.

In my troubled mind I imagine
The world looks like a whirl of the brightest colours ever.
It smells like roses during summer.
It tastes like sweet chocolates.
It makes me feel like I'm free.

And I decide
That I will heal it.

**Sarah Cassady (9)**
Church Drive Primary School, Arnold

## Come On, Save Our World!

Think when you throw rubbish on the floor,
You may be relaxing but it is dangerous for the animals,
So please before you do it, *think!*
If you pollute the sea and the air,
All of nature will die
And once they're dead, they will never come back!
The sea is green,
It is not blue,
The fish are upside down,
Who did it, me and you?
If you're eating a chocolate bar
And can't be bothered to throw it in the bin,
Please still make sure you put it in!
Remember, some people are sitting by the fire,
Drinking a cup of tea,
While some people are as poor as paupers.

**Kiran Kaur (10)**
Church Drive Primary School, Arnold


## Molly's Advice

E veryone listen up! Stop using cars and walk, before the moment fades
A ll of *you* get out of your driving seats and experience the footsteps of goodness
R ed! The Earth is turning red because we're using too much of everything for it to cope with
T he world is spinning fast: time is running out
H aven't any of you noticed that we're actually killing things: plants, animals and even the . . . *Earth?*

**Molly Warrener-Batchelor (10)**
Church Drive Primary School, Arnold

## Heal Our Planet

I'm 0.1%
Barely alive,
Struggling to breathe
And seeping brown goo.
I need help so
What do we need to do?
Save the trees and animals
And help the plants too!
Don't throw litter on the floor!
Help me be happy
*Recycle!*

And I'm getting a bit fitter!
Up to 50%.
Can you tell the world to stop cutting trees down?
A dead plant smells like a rotten egg
And I feel sick inside.

I'm 80% better: good job so far,
Don't stop now though,
I'm not healthy yet.
Just two more things!
Make sure you put the right stuff in the black bin
And in the green bin too!

I'm feeling great:
Bursting with green, glowing with energy.
I'm 100%,
I'm well.
I am *your* Earth.
Thank you.

**Brynn Morris (9)**
Church Drive Primary School, Arnold

## Be A Good Help To The Earth

S *top* right here!
A nimals are suffering
V ans, cars and motorbikes could stop being driven by you today if you wanted to help
E very person can do their little bit to help

O ur world is getting infected because *we* are not taking care to
U se the Earth carefully. It is
R otting slowly, *but* we could put a *stop* to it

E arth is not just yours: think about others
A fter watching TV or playing on the computer, *turn it off!* Don't leave it on standby
R ecycle, start by not throwing litter on the floor
T reat the planet with respect
H elp to create instead of destroy!

**Shaan Kaur (10)**
**Church Drive Primary School, Arnold**

## The Big Green Thing

I'm 0.1%.
Dying, empty.
Don't waste water.
Recycle all of the rubbish.
Please save the world.
Help me please, help me!
Put rubbish in the right bin.
Don't pollute the Earth.
Make me 100%
Healthy, happy.

**Millie Richardson (10)**
**Church Drive Primary School, Arnold**

## Save Me - The World

I feel sad and I need help,
The world is on fire and a mess.
I need your help to recycle litter,
Walk to school or share a ride with some friends.
Turn your lights off, don't leave them on,
Put your rubbish in the bin
Because you can save 100% every day.
Take a quick shower, not a long one,
Stop cutting down trees: you are destroying habitats,
Make sure you turn your taps off: don't leave them on.
If you want the world to be happy, recycle now.
Don't just sit there,
Make the world glad for you and us:
Be eco today and forever.

**Olivia Bragg (9)**
**Church Drive Primary School, Arnold**


## Why It's Good To Recycle

I look outside my window and all I see is grey,
I step outside my door and taste the rotten hay,
I see rubbish on the floor and shout out loud, *'Recycle!'*
Kids throw away needlessly:
And my mind cries.

The next day I see the world much clearer,
And children changing their bad habits.
But all the parents littering,
So the children scream, *'Hey Mum! Recycle!'*
*You* can be the first to shout.
*We can all make a difference!*

**Georgia Kingham (10)**
**Church Drive Primary School, Arnold**

## The Poor World

*'Help! Help! My beautiful world!'*
I am crying.
Dying,
And my whole life is just
Upside down.

Stop.
Think.
*You* need to change our planet.
Stop throwing litter on the floor.
Don't waste food or water.
Animals need looking after
And people need to help.

**Alicia Belshaw (9)**
**Church Drive Primary School, Arnold**

## Recycle

When I was well
I would watch the clouds pass me by
And touch the dandelions being swept along by the wind.
Now,
I am crying because I am dying.
I am getting old.
I need your help to keep me well,
Help me now,
Before I break down.
Stop attacking my heart,
Your poison is starting to hurt.
So end the madness,
Heal me now!

**Connor Skinner (9)**
**Church Drive Primary School, Arnold**

## The Sad Green Planet!

Our planet will begin to cry,
Animals will die,
With the bodies polluted,
Being murdered.

While some people are in warm homes,
Others out in the cold like old garden gnomes.
It makes the world sick,
Like executing a chick.

The planet is almost dead,
Are you using your head?
The planet needs you,
To clean the dirty spew.

If you stop polluting right now,
The planet may recover somehow!

**Holly Wardle (10)**
**Church Drive Primary School, Arnold**


## Our Dying Planet

The ozone disappearing,
The Arctic melting away.
The rainforest has nearly gone:
Animals departing each day,
Breathing in nasty air
And people without food.
But wait. Stop.
What can we children do?
One boy switches off his light
And a girl recycles her clothes.
I shout out, *'Stop the madness!'*
Do *you* hear my message and
Help?

**Dylan Sutcliffe (10)**
**Church Drive Primary School, Arnold**

## Our Big World Needs You!

O ur world was once new
U nder a Heaven full of glowing stars
R esting peacefully, enjoying life

B ig wide world, spinning out there
I s now made of pollution and cries in pain
G enerations of people die

W ith our world like this, *you*
O nly get one chance to
R eally treat it well
L ove it, make the world sing!
D o you want a glorious life?

N ever pollute
E nd this now
E verything you do affects our world
D oes it change your life?
S o make our world a brighter place

Y ou need to stop and recycle
O ur world and people need us
U nder us the world should live, not die.

**Laura Hopewell (10)**
**Church Drive Primary School, Arnold**


## Think

Think,
Can you lend a hand?

I observe bustling cars, smoke seeping out.
I smell scrumptious food that some people won't have.
I listen to the gradually dripping tap, life dripping away.
I sense the Earth's unhurried breath getting slower and slower.

Think,
Can you make a difference
To our fading world?

**Alice Clarke (10)**
**Church Drive Primary School, Arnold**

## Do We Care?

Once there was a polar bear,
It lived on ice that isn't there,
Do we care?

My daddy says he saw a gnu,
Of course it's only in a zoo,
Do we care?

The coral reefs were full of colour,
Now they are boring and much duller,
Do we care?

Plastic floating year after year,
Outlives the people who put it there,
Do we care?

Fumes from cars in the air,
Pollution is everywhere,
Do we care?

**Amy Evans (8)**
**East Markham Primary School, East Markham**


## Why Waste Petrol?

Why always go in the car
When walking can get you very far?
Travelling in the car is bad for you,
Try walking and do something new!

Cars, cars everywhere!
Pollution, pollution, travelling in the air.
Going in the car is wasting time,
Walking is absolutely fine!

Stop wasting money, why waste it
When you can walk and get fit?
Why make such a polluted mess
When surely walking is the best?

**Katie Whelan (10)**
**East Markham Primary School, East Markham**

## The Earth Is Good, The Earth Is Bad

The Earth is good, the Earth is bad,
Bad things happen, like war,
That's bad,
Litter, rainforests being cut down,
Homeless people in deserted towns.

Disease gets spread and can't be dealt with,
As medication is lost, not found,
Many people starve every day,
So think about them
And wish to help all the starving people when you pray.

People die because there is no fresh water,
So think about that,
Because one of them could be someone's daughter.
If you don't, you're likely to regret it some day,
They don't even have proper beds,
Just ones made out of straw and hay.
You could help them and if you do,
You're making someone as lucky as *you!*
Another reason why you should
Is because for them it would be a dream come true.

They don't have proper houses,
Not even ones made of bricks,
Just ones made of straw like their beds,
Which are easily destroyed.
Everything in it completely destroyed,
But what can they do about it?
They don't have the money to get everything fixed,
But they might have fancy football tricks.

They do have love and each other,
But some don't even have a mother.
So compared to them, you are really lucky,
You have got a really safe home,
*Unlike them!*

**Isaac Higgs (9)**
**East Markham Primary School, East Markham**

## Litter

L ittering can kill animals, if they eat it, they might choke and die
I t kills the environment by making it look a mess
and some plastic bags don't rot in five hundred years
T idy up after you use rubbish and put it in the bin
T idying helps the environment because it doesn't get in our way
E nvironment is being destroyed partly by littering
R ecycling is also good because you're not using so many gases.

**George Thorne (10)**
East Markham Primary School, East Markham

## Being Homeless

Being homeless is terrible,
You barely get any food.
You have to find a place on the streets
To sleep every night.
People have tarmac
Instead of a mattress.
They have two rags
Instead of a quilt.
Think, if you ever see someone
On the streets,
If you have any money,
Just give them a bit.
Doesn't matter how much,
Just a bit.

**Daniel Gagg (11)**
East Markham Primary School, East Markham

## Endangered Animals

When the same type of animal is killed too many times,
Eventually the species will soon die.
This is called extinction, the animal will go,
This is what happened to the great bird dodo.

Some animals are not extinct but very close to it,
Some animals are not extinct, just a little bit.
These animals are harmless, they must survive,
They are put in special places just to stay alive!

Many, many years ago, hunting was a sport,
Elephants were hunted, for their lives they fought!
The hunters took their ivory, all of it was bought,
Piano keys were ivory, but not anymore.

**Derek Milton (10)**
**East Markham Primary School, East Markham**


## Green World

The world may look like this
If you just help the world!
But the best part is, no pollution,
Nothing bad at all.
People have a smile on their face,
No crime or stealing,
It just made me think,
Our world just might look like that,
If you just *help!*

**Lucy Garnett (9)**
**East Markham Primary School, East Markham**

# Rubbish

Rubbish, rubbish, when you don't put it in the bin,
You are committing a really bad sin.
It's polluting the world more and more,
When you drop rubbish on the floor.

Rubbish, rubbish, don't bury it in the ground,
Because another way of recycling could still be found.
Next time, instead of throwing things away,
Try and use them another way.

So go out into the world
And pick up litter that people have hurled.
What are you waiting for?
This is an important case,
Go and make this planet a cleaner place.

**Alexander Ridgway (9)**
**East Markham Primary School, East Markham**


# The Flood

The ice caps are melting
The rain is pelting
Temperature is rising
So the flood is coming.

People are dying
Of heat and starvation
Together we can help them
Live a better life.

Why do we litter?
We want to be healthier
So why don't we stop it
And end this thing?

**Kyle Smith (11)**
**East Markham Primary School, East Markham**

## Imagine

Imagine how you would feel
Not having a home to go to.
Imagine if you were sleeping on the streets.
Where would you go? What would you do?
Imagine feeling lost and unwanted.
Imagine if someone turned you down and said no.
Having torn clothes and hoping, praying for food.
Imagine if you could just hear a friendly hello.
Imagine . . .

Imagine - what can you do?
You see rubbish everywhere you go.
There's litter all around you,
Surrounding you there's litter.
What do you do?
Sweet wrappers, crisp packets, bottles and cans,
People ignoring the bins - it's like saying no!
Make people listen, make it stop!
Just imagine a clean world.

**Lauren Gardiner (11)**
**East Markham Primary School, East Markham**


## Animals

Animals are cute, some can be bad,
If you ignore them, they will always be sad.

Some animals are cute, some animals are fluffy,
But I always think, they're always lovely.

I think that I'm a killer, for the food we always eat,
They are all animals, but it does taste unique.

Some animals are wild, some animals are pets,
I have a guinea pig, a tortoise and a dog.
They're my favourites and the best.

**Amy-Sue Johnson (9)**
**East Markham Primary School, East Markham**

# What Can We Do?

War is dreadful, mean and unkind,
The gunshots, the bombs dropped.
War is blood and death,
The friends, the family.
What can we do?

Litter is disgraceful,
The carrier bags, the Coke cans.
Litter is ridiculous,
There's a bin right over there.
What can we do?

Climate change is worrying,
The really hot winters, the really cold summers.
Climate change is bad,
The ice that melts, the sea that rises,
What can we do?

Being homeless is scary,
The nights are dark, the sun is hot.
Being homeless is no picnic,
The ground is hard, the bugs that fly around.
What can we do?

Animals need our help,
The fur, the tusks, the meat.
Animals need to be saved,
The dodo never had a chance.
What can we do?

Think of peace,
Think of cleanliness,
Think of normal weather,
Think of homes around the world,
Think of animals.

All of this is scary,
You never know what might happen.
Now it's up to you!

**Lauren Norman (11)**
East Markham Primary School, East Markham


## Why?

Why is there litter scattering the lane?
Why is there disease causing people pain?

Why is there war that makes people afraid?
Why is there homelessness just because the rent cannot be paid?

Why do terrorists murder and kill?
Why are there robbers that take money from the till?

Why can't some people recycle and use things twice?
Why are rainforests cut down? It's just not nice!

Why is there poverty, so there's not enough food?
Why are some people unhelpful and why are some people rude?

Why is there pollution? Maybe because of the cars?
Why are animals becoming extinct?
And why are butterflies suffocated in a jar?
I wish that all these things didn't happen. *But they do!*

But what can we do to make this world a better place to live?
A little help and thoughtfulness is all that you need to give!

**Sarah Eakin (9)**
East Markham Primary School, East Markham

# Sense The Change

What can I smell?
I smell war.
The shot of a gun, the smoke of a bomb.
I smell blood and death,
This has got to end.

What can I see?
I see litter.
Crisp packets everywhere, gum lining the floor.
I see cans and plastic,
This has got to end.

What can I hear?
I hear racism.
Nasty, spiteful words, people hurt and afraid.
I hear whispers and shouts,
This has got to end.

What can I feel?
I feel pollution.
Smoke blackening the sky, car fumes choking me.
I feel the pollution all around,
This has got to end.

What can I taste?
I taste disease.
The cries for help, infections spreading.
I taste dirt and filth,
This has got to end.

I smell war,
I see litter,
I hear racism,
I touch pollution,
I taste disease.
Working together,
We can change this.

I smell fresh air,
I see clean streets,
I hear kind words,
I touch new green grass,
I taste natural food.
It has been changed.

**Megan Eakin (11)**
East Markham Primary School, East Markham

## The World

Warning, warning, warning,
Be careful of the global warming.
The world is a big disgrace,
So how could we make it a better place?

We can see litter from bottles to cans,
We also get pollution from cars to vans.
The world, it's a big disgrace,
So how can we make a better place?

Why must animals be killed with a lot of pain?
Why do hunters kill them? They do it for money to gain.
The world is a big disgrace,
So how could we make it a better place?

How can we stop it? Well that's easy,
Put things in the bin, if you don't want it messy.
Maybe if we picked up the pace,
The world would be a better place.

**Lewis Foley (10)**
East Markham Primary School, East Markham

## Global Warning!

Did you know the world might burn?
And it's all under our concern,
Because of our pollution,
The whole world will go out of motion.

We are creating carbon dioxide,
Which causes the sun's heat to be magnified,
Which makes our world all hot
And burns us up, so live we will not.

So instead of driving your car,
Walk if you don't have to go far,
Switch off the light to save energy,
Stop the ice caps melting warmly.

You really have to get set,
If you want to save the planet.
If we all help stop global warming
It becomes not such a global warning.

**George Shaw (10)**
**East Markham Primary School, East Markham**


## Pollution

I was driving my car through the night,
While smoke was ruining wildlife.

'When will this pollution stop?'
Said the rabbit in a hop.

'I hope it stops soon,'
Said the stars and the moon.

'Will humans ever be told?'
Said a hedgehog feeling bold.

'Next time I think I will ride my bike,'
Said I with a fright.

**Ellie Clarson (8)**
**East Markham Primary School, East Markham**

## Poppies On The Battlefield

Years ago there was an invasion of a country,
But they fought back and the world went to war.
The sound of guns terrified the soldiers,
Who shot and ran, fighting for their lives.

The fields and meadows were all churned up
And trenches were dug, leaving nothing but mud.
The wind and the rain poured down on the Earth,
But when all hope was lost, a poppy grew on the battlefield.

The flowers gave the soldiers strength
And when Hitler surrendered, the soldiers went home.
The men that died brought home nothing but devastation to
                                                                 their families,

The product of war.

The wars of today have the same products,
Devastation and sadness for the families of the men
Who have fallen in wars.

**Jack Higgs (11)**
**East Markham Primary School, East Markham**


## Recycle

R emember - recycle all that you can
E verything, including that old steel pan!
C olours of glass all waiting to bank
Y ou can always rely on that smashing clank!
C onsider the planet, we need to take care
L et's all recycle and show we're aware!
E veryone should *recycle!*

**Sophie Finch (8)**
**East Markham Primary School, East Markham**

## Reduce, Reuse, Recycle

Recycling is good,
Recycling is ace,
You can do it to food,
You can do it to waste.

Recycling is great,
Recycling is cool,
It can be your mate,
Unless you're a fool.

Recycling is helpful,
Recycling is fantastic,
Recycling is thoughtful,
Recycling is magic.

Recycling helps the countryside,
Recycling helps bees,
Recycling is worldwide,
Recycling helps trees.

**Emily Holmes (9)**
**East Markham Primary School, East Markham**

## Nothing To Gain But Pain

Homeless people with disease,
Living in a world of pollution,
Most have nits and fleas,
All they need is our contribution.

People in pain,
Living on the streets and country lanes,
Nothing to gain
But pain.

Some have too much sun, some have too much rain,
Eating the same,
Nothing to gain
But pain.

But we can make it better,
Give them water to drink,
Or to make their crops wetter,
Just think!

**Laura Beckett (10)**
**East Markham Primary School, East Markham**

## Hugging The World

In some countries there's pollution,
But in fact there's a solution.
Not everyone will care,
That there's pollution in the air.
Some things are really sad,
Like the hungry people in Trinidad.

Save your water we all pray,
Use all your paper every day.
This means use every side,
Donate money to far and wide.
Sharing your car is very nice,
This is really good advice.

Please walk to school,
This is a good rule.
Using a bike is even more fast,
Don't waste food, make it last.
If riding a motorbike, this will help you,
It's much faster, less petrol is used too.

Care for people, animals and trees,
Think of the people over the seas.
The world cares for us,
Give the world a hug!

**Emily Davies (10)**
**East Markham Primary School, East Markham**

# The World At Risk

Have you ever thought about pollution?
If you walk instead of drive,
You could keep the world alive.
You may not think there is any point,
But do you think there is a special ointment?
Small things make a huge difference.

You know that thing called poverty?
Through Action Aid, you can sponsor a child like Dorothy.
Dorothy is only eight, she never gets a plate of food,
Her whole country is in a whole mess.
When you go on holiday,
Do you ever see homelessness, poverty?
These people need help.
Stop and get them a drink or food,
Don't walk past and be rude.
Give them money or give them food,
You've seen it on the news, do something about it.
*Save the world!*

**Jake Casburn (11)**
**East Markham Primary School, East Markham**

## The Horrors Of Global Warming

A million cars and lorries,
Spreading this awful disease
And no, I am not talking about the ones
Where you just cough and sneeze.

For the ozone barrier is breaking away
And soon all the polar bears will have to pay,
For our costly mistake that we all made.

And every second, every minute, every day and year,
A tiny piece of ice just disappears.
There's one little thing that we can do,
Don't take the car, just recycle
And you will be saving a mass of life cycles
And then you will be making a big difference!

**Matthew Steels (11)**
**East Markham Primary School, East Markham**


## Why Waste?

Petrol wasting is so bad,
Walking, walking will make you glad.
Better walking than sitting in a car,
Walking, walking will get you far.

Stop wasting money,
When you could get very fit,
Running around the block,
While time goes tick-tick.

Pollution, pollution in your hair,
Pollution, pollution thickens the air.

**Danielle Cosgrove (10)**
**East Markham Primary School, East Markham**

## Poverty

P oor people in Africa
O ver every hill and mountain, people searching for food
V ery hungry people everywhere
E ating if they're lucky
R ags are what they wear, for all they can afford is nothing
T atty houses are what they live in
Y ou can make a difference.

**Bethany Ashmore (7)**
**Fairmeadows Foundation Primary School, Newhall**


## Stop!

Pollution should *stop!*
*Stop* going in the car,
Try to walk instead.
*Stop* all the exhaust fumes,
Try to take a bus.
*Stop! Stop! Stop!*

**Tamzin Irvine-Brentnall (8)**
**Fairmeadows Foundation Primary School, Newhall**


## War

W ar is scary and frightening
A ll people fighting each other
R ed blood spilt everywhere.

**Joshua Smith (8)**
**Fairmeadows Foundation Primary School, Newhall**

## Animals And Extinction

I don't think it is fair!
Animals should not be killed.
They are God's creatures.
Why do people kill animals?
If we don't stop killing, they will become extinct!
Would you like to live in a world without animals?

**Kayleigh Ison (8)**
**Fairmeadows Foundation Primary School, Newhall**


## A World Without Animals

Why do we have to kill animals?
Soon they will become extinct.
You're always taking their fur away.
Would you like it if you were them? I wouldn't.
Would you like to live in a world without animals?

**Elly-Mae Griffiths (8)**
**Fairmeadows Foundation Primary School, Newhall**


## Litter

Litter makes me angry.
I put my litter in my bin.
People should pick up rubbish
And recycle!

**Kiara Knight (8)**
**Fairmeadows Foundation Primary School, Newhall**

## Stop This Pollution

P lease stop this pollution!
O ur world needs animals
L ovely fish swimming in the sea
L ots of shiny fish in the water
U sually I hear birds on the way to school
T alking to each other
I don't think it's fair that we are killing the animals!
O ur world will be sad when there are no animals left
N ow it's time to stop this pollution.

**Kaytlin Dyche (8)**
**Fairmeadows Foundation Primary School, Newhall**


## Litter

L itter is disgusting
I t makes me bitter
T ake it to a bin
T ake it home
E at food, don't turn it into litter
R ecycle!

**Caitlin Rees (8)**
**Fairmeadows Foundation Primary School, Newhall**


## Wars

What are wars?
Wars are dangerous.
Risking lives to make a better world.
Are you ready to fight?

**Brandon Hook (8)**
**Fairmeadows Foundation Primary School, Newhall**

## Poverty

P oor people in Africa
O ver all of Africa
V ery hungry people
E ating if they can
R ags are all they wear
T ravelling miles for water
Y oung children dying every minute.

**India Oakey (7)**
**Fairmeadows Foundation Primary School, Newhall**


## War!

W ar is not nice, it kills
A ll risking lives
R ed poppies for Remembrance Day
    to remember our grandads who died in the war.

**Reece Clamp (8)**
**Fairmeadows Foundation Primary School, Newhall**


## War!

W ar is not fair
A ll people die and people cry
R emember, war is despicable!

**Amber Ottaway (8)**
**Fairmeadows Foundation Primary School, Newhall**


## War

W ar is evil
A war kills people
R est in peace, soldiers.

**Joseph Hyde (7)**
**Fairmeadows Foundation Primary School, Newhall**

## Litter!

L itter, litter makes me bitter
I t makes me mad
T hrow litter in the bin
T ry to stay clean
E verywhere there are litterbugs
R ecycle more litter.

**Zak Morris (7)**
**Fairmeadows Foundation Primary School, Newhall**


## The Tiger

Tigers are becoming extinct,
Trees are being cut down,
No trees in the jungle,
Where can the tiger live?

**Kane Clamp (7)**
**Fairmeadows Foundation Primary School, Newhall**


## My Poem About War

I think war should stop forever.
We all know we are as good as each other.
Let boys and girls live together.

**Luke Wadsworth (8)**
**Fairmeadows Foundation Primary School, Newhall**


## My Poem About Litter

Litter makes me turn bitter,
Put it in a rocket and send it to Miss Locket.
Miss Locket put it in her pocket,
Fritter a piece of litter.

**Mollie Moon (7)**
**Fairmeadows Foundation Primary School, Newhall**

## Pollution

P lease don't kill animals in the water
O ur world would be sad without fish
L ovely fish swimming in the sea
L eave the fish to swim
U nusual fish try to get away
T aking fish by fish
I think it's not fair
O ur world needs animals
N ice fish swimming in the sea.

**Sophie McMahon (7)**
**Fairmeadows Foundation Primary School, Newhall**


## Pollution Needs A Solution

The sky will go black,
The sun will go down,
Well, isn't that going to happen,
When you're driving around?

You're killing yourselves,
You might not be able to see
And if you carry on driving,
You'll end up killing me.

The rain will not fall,
The grasslands will be gone,
Innocent people will die,
As they have no world to live upon.

They are your warnings,
You are advised to listen now,
So come on, work together
And we can turn our world around.

**Emma Sunderland (10)**
**Heymann Primary School, West Bridgford**

## Help This Tree!

There is a terrified bird sitting in a tree,
It's getting cut down just for you and me.
It's been cut down with a big, sharp knife,
Now that tree has no life.
Why did that tree have to go?
I guess that man did not know,
How important trees are to us
And all of this is just because,
A selfish man wanted a piece of paper
To not even use and throw away later.
Oh please, oh please,
Stop bullying these trees.
Just help them survive
And stay alive.

**Hania Hickling (10)**
**Heymann Primary School, West Bridgford**


## Pollution And Trees

The air is dirty,
When we're doing thirty,
In my Mini,
With my friend Vinnie.

Rainforests are being cut down,
And now they sell the wood in town.
We need the trees to breathe,
So then we can achieve,
Saving the trees,
And maybe the leaves.

**Daniel Hardy (11)**
**Heymann Primary School, West Bridgford**

## Turtles Vs Packaging!

I am a turtle, I live in the sea,
I breed on shore but my young are not safe.
They are losing their lives because of you.

We want our children to be free,
We want to be free,
Our lives are in danger,
Because of the nets, the rubbish and waste.

You make us angry, the people who don't care,
You people who created this monstrosity,
So please let us live our lives in peace,
Please! Please! Please!

**Matthew Quayle (11)**
**Heymann Primary School, West Bridgford**


## Hotter World

Pollution causes the Earth to get hotter,
A scorcher and what a terrible thing that is!
With the world in a twist,
Of tornadoes and cyclones.

The Earth was made to be good,
So surely everyone could
Make a sacrifice to be nice
To the world.

**Joshua Lee (11)**
**Heymann Primary School, West Bridgford**

## What Has Happened?

The rain is not falling,
Clean water running out,
The birds are all calling,
For no more of this drought.

Is there any hope,
For those who care?
We are slipping down the biggest slope
The world will ever share.

Forests have been cut down,
Birds have lost their place,
There are too many cars in town,
What's happened to the human race?

**Lydia Williams (11)**
**Heymann Primary School, West Bridgford**


## Pollution

Aeroplanes fly right above the clouds,
Making a sound that's very loud.
It wakes us up when we are asleep,
Like an alarm clock that goes *beep, beep.*

Cars have exhaust pipes that have smoke in them,
Affecting people because it's spreading in the air.
We have a big fight on
And we pay the price.

**Owais Hussain (10)**
**Heymann Primary School, West Bridgford**

## Our Endangered World

The environment is a very special place to us
Because of all the things it does.
Our world is going to end up like a bin,
So quickly put yourself in someone else's skin.

Help the forest with all of its needs,
If the animals could talk they would all plead.
The big, the small, the ever so tall,
We all feel the same way about how we treat the world today.

Why do we fill the sea with pollution
When I can give you a better solution?
Now all we need to do
Is create a new world or a new you!

**Sophie Turner (11)**
Heymann Primary School, West Bridgford


## The Cold Ice

All the ice is slippery
Though I can still feel the breeze
Watch as it all melts.
The sun shines on the ice
So we don't have any fun
The water has got higher.
I can still feel the cold ice on my foot
My boot is full of ice
Ice all gone
By my sight it hasn't gone right.

**Jaskaran Kaur (11)**
Heymann Primary School, West Bridgford

## Save It Soon

The environment is a very special place,
It keeps alive the human race.
We're always making such a fuss,
That life isn't good enough for us.
The world just now, it is a bin,
Try going in someone else's skin.
You could switch off the lights, computers, TVs,
After you've used them, I'm asking you please.
Climate changes like flipping over book pages,
Use less electricity, you'll have more wages.
This day to day basis will help you a lot,
Even though you don't know it,
The world is getting too hot.

**Catriona Higgins (11)**
**Heymann Primary School, West Bridgford**


## Oil

Oh how I wish to swim again,
To sing love songs,
To linger behind my mum.
Mum, where are you when I need you?
Why can't I be with you?

To love and cherish this day,
For I have not seen a single oil ship in sight,
At last we are free, they say.
But I fear not, as I will see an oil ship another day.
Jim - The Whale.

**Didi Sadeq (11)**
**Heymann Primary School, West Bridgford**

## Animal Cruelty

We all like to see animals in the zoo,
But what do we think of this idea?
A good one or a bad one?
We can see lions, tigers and deer.
Wouldn't we want to see them in the wild?
It won't be long before they're extinct.
Poaching killed the dodo.
Bears acting like clowns.
Tarantulas kept as pets.
Oh why don't we try?
It won't be long before they're all gone.
It's such a pointless idea.

**Tom Polkinghorne (11)**
**Heymann Primary School, West Bridgford**


## The Big Green Poem

Change your way,
Then the Earth can stay,
Great and powerful every day.

Hurry up,
Time is short,
Time is fading away.

The pollution is coming,
So get running,
Time is gone,
So be strong.

You should have changed your ways,
Then the Earth would have stayed
Lovely and beautiful every day!

**Stephanie Dewan (11)**
**Heymann Primary School, West Bridgford**

## Save Our World

The world is a very delicate place,
It is home to the human race.
But how long for do you think?
It might be gone in just a blink.

The world is a ball of glass,
Just about to smash.
There are lots of things we can do,
To help our world see this through.

Recycling is just one of the things,
To stop our world from becoming a bin.
You will be surprised what recycling does,
So sit down and listen because,

The world is a ball of glass,
Just about to smash,
Think of all the people dying,
I bet you they'll die crying.

Yes, you should blame yourself,
It's everyone's fault.

**Rhia Moore (11)**
**Heymann Primary School, West Bridgford**


## The Landfill Site Is . . .

The landfill site is a foul rubbish mountain.
The stench in the air is as disgusting as a sewer.
The sky is dark with impending doom,
The rotted rats bring death like creeping cancer in the air.
Can anyone save the world from disaster,
Or is it a challenge no one can master?
The landfill dump is a heartbreaking sight,
We must try harder to make it right.

**Michael Butcher (11)**
**Heymann Primary School, West Bridgford**

# Change Your Ways

If you want this Earth to stay,
Be friendly to the environment
And change your ways.

There are five simple ways to reduce $CO_2$,
You can switch off electrical items
When they are not in use.

Recycle items such as plastic and glass,
You never know,
It could be used in your class.

Save some water, don't be a fool,
You could save enough to fill
An Olympic-sized swimming pool.

Do not litter, don't let off methane,
Protect your environment
And don't be insane.

Don't keep driving, try to walk,
Or maybe cycle.
Action is better than talk.

If you want this Earth to stay,
Be friendly to the environment
And change your ways!

**Gurpreet Sehmbi (11)**
**Heymann Primary School, West Bridgford**

## The Landfill Site

The people's heads are bowed like dead daffodils
Blowing in the breeze,
There's nothing there, no life, no trees,
How can we help this putrid place?
It is a disgrace to the human race.

The booming bulldozers drive with thunderous wheels,
The people are scavenging for their meals.
There's one simple thing that I ask you to do,
Don't throw away uneaten food.

Put yourself in someone else's shoes,
You will be surprised by what they do.
It is not pretty, it is not bright,
It is not good for our environment,
Yes, we will fight!

We will stop this nonsense here and now,
Just please tell me how.
I want to know, I want to help,
Nothing happens when we yelp!
I love the world, so do you,
There are many things we can do.
So renew the world, renew yourself,
It will help the world and help your health.

**Hannah Shepheard (11)**
**Heymann Primary School, West Bridgford**

## Health Warning!

Do you want this to happen?
The disgraceful sight of rats rummaging through trash.
The sound of booming bulldozers battering, mish mash.
The smell, as disgusting as a mountain of sick.
The taste in the air is as though you've been kicked.

So what can you do to avoid this disgrace?
Surely the answers staring right in your face?
Recycle your rubbish, starve the rats.
Abandon the monsters that carve up the land.
Go green for a far more pleasant perfume.
Light up your lives, grow out of the gloom!

**Azeem Razak (11)**
**Heymann Primary School, West Bridgford**


## Save It

Cars go round, pumping fuel into the air,
For the animals around us, this clearly isn't fair.
The world was once a peaceful place, no pollution at all,
It's time you realised; the world isn't a steel ball.
Trees are the main part of nature, they allow us to breathe,
But you'd better be aware, before you know it they may leave.

**Mark Webster (11)**
**Heymann Primary School, West Bridgford**

## The Polluted Ocean

The ocean is home to thousands of creatures,
Full of fantastic, fascinating features.
So why do we fill it with lots of pollution?
We can give you a better solution.

Don't sit there with your hands on your laps,
Reduce the amount of carrier bags.
Recycle, reduce and reproduce,
All the stuff you like to use.
So think this over once or twice,
The government will think you're really nice.

**Pavandeep Lakhanpal (11)**
**Heymann Primary School, West Bridgford**


## Help

Animals' habitats are put in danger,
Why don't you become an environment ranger?
Lock all the pollution inside a wooden crate,
Help save the world before it's too late!
Global warming is getting worse,
Help make this better like an environment nurse.

**Michael Lamb (11)**
**Heymann Primary School, West Bridgford**

## Forest Friend Or Foe?

The forest was where I used to live
And then came along a 'div'.
He cut down all I know,
Even the home of the sweet dodo.

Gorillas, ocelots, tigers and snakes,
All liked to feed in the local lakes.
Most of the animals died you see,
Though I was strong and lived. That's me!

More of this treatment and I'll die,
For all I've found to eat so far is a dead fly.
So when you're washing your face in a sink,
Make sure you give me, jaguar, a think.

**Victoria Tantum (11)**
**Heymann Primary School, West Bridgford**


## Help!

Ice caps, icebergs and other things,
All of them melting, it really stings,
Especially animals like penguins.

Turn off the taps and the TVs,
Do what I say, I am begging you, please.
If you do, you'll save electricity
And ensure the Earth's sustainability.

**Oli Kitt (11)**
**Heymann Primary School, West Bridgford**

## Differences

Waving, washing, whimpering,
The sounds of the ocean echo,
Crystal clear, blue water,
At a calm, steady tempo.
Calling, colossal, colourful,
The lush green canopy is breathtaking,
Subtle tones blending,
New life is waking.
Dirty, disgusting, disappointing,
The fumes waft away in the air,
Plants and trees are dying,
Like this, we will get nowhere.
Rotting, rushing, rumbling,
The world cannot be saved by one man,
Soon the Earth will be too tired to cope
And it will go, as it came, with a *bang!*

**Hassiba Boukari (11)**
**Heymann Primary School, West Bridgford**


## The Ice

I'm going to melt, I'm going to destroy
So do your bit.
Reduce the gases coming from you
Because of you we have to suffer.
All we ask is that you reduce the gases you are making
And reduce your carbon footprint.

**Alana Lowe (10)**
**Heymann Primary School, West Bridgford**

## Old Tree's Words

For hundreds of years I've stood here, watching time fly by,
But in all those years, nothing was like what now lies in front of
                                                          my eyes.
Where once flowers grew, rubbish clutters the path,
A few surviving plants now trapped in pollution's wrath.
All animals, great and small, used to have a home,
With all their habitats now gone, they have nowhere to roam.
Before, the weather was fair, pleasantly gentle and mild,
But what about now? It's crazy, unpredictable and wild.
Children long ago played nicely, all had a lovely time,
Now hooligans strut around on streets, sniffing around for crime.
All the 'amazing' new gadgets were never heard of then,
Now, materials used, products made, just to follow the latest trend.
What is happening? What's going on? Does anybody care?
Everybody, please! Help our world and everybody and
                                                    everything there.

**Lulu Song (11)**
**Heymann Primary School, West Bridgford**


## Many Different Ways To Save The Earth!

The green Earth turns in 365 days,
We can save the planet in so many different ways!

Everyone here can help save the world,
Never give up - take my word!

Very little energy it takes, to put some effort in,
If everyone helps we can save the world within!

Throw your litter in the bin,
Let's save the world for our next of kin!

All the smoke that pollutes the air,
Don't make fires, show that you care!

**Zoe Tissington (11)**
**Holly Hill Primary School, Selston**

## Reuse, Reduce, Recycle

Reuse, reduce, recycle - make the world great,
There will be nothing left of the Earth at this rate!
Don't drop litter, put it in the bins,
Recycle your paper, cardboard and tins!
Reuse your bags, pots and paper,
Do it now, not later!
Reduce the pollution, fumes and smoke,
If we don't, soon we will all choke!
So make a difference today,
We will soon save the planet . . . *hooray!*

**Eleanor Sewell (11)**
**Holly Hill Primary School, Selston**


## This Is Your Green Life!

I often wonder how it is,
That on a lovely day,
Lots of things which need to change,
Below, is when I say . . .

Big smoke is in the air,
When I'm walking all around,
It harms and acts horribly,
In our precious eco town!

We have to save the water,
It is a pleasing sight,
Turning off *all* the taps,
Is really, really right!

I really wish we all turn green,
It seems so very right,
For when I look and see the world,
It's not a pretty sight!

**Ross Whyatt (10)**
**Holly Hill Primary School, Selston**

## The Big Green World

*(By recycling one glass bottle and having a quick shower, you save enough energy to power a TV for three hours)*

G reen
R euse, reduce, recycle
E verlasting planet
E nvironmentally friendly
N ever-ending world

W aste no more
O ur world is important
R escue the Earth
L eaking oil
D estined to be a better home, Earth

Now just listen,
Here is the hint,
Reuse, reduce, recycle,
To reduce your carbon footprint.

**Georgia Culligan (11)**
**Holly Hill Primary School, Selston**


## Save The World

The air is bad,
It makes me sad,
We're surrounded by smoke,
It's making us choke,
Due to war,
People are poor,
Try to make pollution stop
And the Earth will not pop,
Water waste,
Is a disgrace!

**Katie Moss (11)**
**Holly Hill Primary School, Selston**

## War

Bombs are arriving,
People start dying.
England and America are under attack,
Everyone is scared because Hitler's back.
Sirens make a sound,
As people flee underground,
Parents are saying goodbye,
'Cause the children don't want to die.
We are trying to stop the war,
Because everyone is getting poor.

**Mia Maciejewski (11)**
**Holly Hill Primary School, Selston**


## Help The Planet!

H elp the planet!
E arth is dying,
L ittle by little,
P overty is arriving.

T he Earth is hotter,
H elp! Ice is melting,
E verything will be destroyed!

P eople are starting wars,
L iving in despair,
A ll will soon be dead,
N othing left,
E verything gone,
T he Earth is over!

**Beth Moss (11)**
**Holly Hill Primary School, Selston**

## Save The World

S ave our world!
A nimals are becoming extinct
V ictoriously help us save them
E xtinction is here!

T he climate is changing
H elp stop ice melting
E veryone, stop global warming!

W ar is starting
O ver the world
R aiding all the countries
L iving in agony, people suffer
D ying every day!

    Help save our planet . . . *now!*
    Everyone can do something. Take action!

**Jade Fantom (11)**
**Holly Hill Primary School, Selston**


## Recycling World

R ecycle
E verlasting world
C leaning the planet
Y ou can do it
C utting down on landfills
L iving ever longer
E veryone can do it!

**Nathan Dudley (11)**
**Holly Hill Primary School, Selston**

## Green Machine

G oing green is so cool
R educe, reuse, recycle
E ver-ending world
E co-friendly
N ever lasting world

M ake your own compost
A ssist your workmates
C lean the planet
H elping the plants
I ncrease the amount of the three Rs
N ever give up
E veryone go green!

**Clara Gray (11)**
Holly Hill Primary School, Selston


## Save Our Planet

R ecycle please!
E nvironmentally friendly cars
C ut down on waste
Y our world, look after it!
C reatures matter
L itter spoils the Earth
E nergy save, please!
   All these would make the Earth
   A better place to live if we recycle!

**Danielle Stevenson (11)**
Holly Hill Primary School, Selston

# The Three Rs

Many people waste their paper,
Here and everywhere!
So more trees are chopped down,
Decreasing the oxygen in the air!

It would be better to walk,
Than to ride in the car!
Especially if your journey,
Isn't really that far!

Litter, litter,
It is like a bug!
It steals our world,
Like an evil thug!

Recycle your paper,
It will do the Earth good.
It will also save the trees
From crashing in the mud!

Reduce the use of your car
And walk, skip and sprint!
It can save the planet
And reduce your carbon footprint!

Reuse your litter,
Such as bottles and cans.
Tell your family and friends,
Including your nans!

**Emma Trower (10)**
**Holly Hill Primary School, Selston**

## Worrying Wars!

The war is so bad,
I'm feeling so sad.
Due to the war,
We can't go out the door.
People are dying,
That's why we're crying.
Rations are flowing,
Cities are blowing.
The sky is black,
We're under attack.
I surrender, don't shoot,
Please, I'm being cute.
Britain has won,
We can now see the sun.
Hooray! Hooray!
We've saved the day!

**Brady Tagg (10)**
**Holly Hill Primary School, Selston**


## Litter

Rubbish releaser
Wrapper dropper
Gum spitter
Pollution maker
Planet killer.

**Jessica Davidson (10)**
**Kingswood Primary School, Corby**

# Litterbug

Food thrower
Wrapper dropper
Litter sprinkler
Gum spitter
Wall destroyer
Paper flinger
Dog messer
Mess maker
Graffiti drawer
Planet destroyer.

**Georgia Hargin (9)**
Kingswood Primary School, Corby


# Litterbug

Litter dropper
Gum spitter
Glass smasher
Mess maker
Animal killer
Planet destroyer.

**George Blackie (9)**
Kingswood Primary School, Corby


# Litter

Wrapper dropper
Gum spitter
Glass smasher
Litter releaser
Ozone destroyer
Animal killer
Planet destroyer!

**Anita Ullah (10)**
Kingswood Primary School, Corby

## Peace

It was night and very bright,
The world was calm and quiet,
Happy people in their beds,
Resting their sleepy heads.
I hope they're having a wonderful dream,
Having peace is what it means.

**Robyn Smith (9)**
Kingswood Primary School, Corby

## War

Mass murderer
Family destroyer
Heart breaker
Orphan maker
Man killer
Village wrecker
Death bringer.

**Samantha Matthews (11)**
Kingswood Primary School, Corby

## Litter

Smelly
Harms animals
Everywhere is a mess
Take your litter home
Recycle rubbish.

**Kelseylea Burgess (9)**
Kingswood Primary School, Corby

## I Have A Dream

I have a dream,
That people won't litter and destroy our planet.
People are the murderers
And Earth is the victim.
However, we are also the judges of our actions.

I have a dream,
That poverty will be non-existent,
That all the wars are over.
So families can be reunited
And people won't lose their lives.

I have a dream,
That people of a different race won't argue,
Because we are all the same,
So there is no need for discrimination.

These dreams can come true,
If we all unite as one.
We can fight for the right of our world,
People and countries,
To make the world safe and friendly.

**Sai Stephenson (11)**
**Kingswood Primary School, Corby**


## Extinction - Haikus

Killing for fashion
White tigers are in danger
We destroy tigers

Help stop cruelty
Prevent tigers being shot
To reduce life loss.

**James Ingram (11)**
**Kingswood Primary School, Corby**

## Save The Environment!

Because of the pollution,
The rainforest is dead,
The animals will be extinct,
So we won't get fed.

We all should recycle,
To help save the nation,
So get rid of all the litter,
Then we won't be in a terrible situation.

Save the environment,
Make it a better place,
Recycle all the rubbish,
So we don't live in disgrace.

**Abigail Storrie (10)**
**Kingswood Primary School, Corby**


## War

Gun shooter
Gas maker
Sword fighter
Village burner
Family destroyer
Village wrecker
Bomb maker
Heart breaker
Lost limbs
Child evacuator
Orphan producer
People killer
Child killer.

**Courtney Cook (10)**
**Kingswood Primary School, Corby**

## Litter

Please don't litter, I plead, I beg,
The world's full of rubbish, it's full of disgrace.
Please don'' litter, I plead, I beg,
If you clean up your act, the world will be a better place.

Please don't litter, I plead, I beg,
Think of the animals dying in pain.
Please don't litter, I plead, I beg,
Dropping your rubbish you have nothing to gain.

**Christopher Hart (11)**
**Kingswood Primary School, Corby**

## Animals Rock!

A nimals shouldn't be harmed
N o hunting and killing
I 'll love my pets forever
M y animals rock
A wild animal isn't scary
L ove, care, food and drink
S o love your animal before extinction!

**Kieran McNairn (9)**
**Kingswood Primary School, Corby**

## Litter

Gum spitter,
Planet destroyer,
Litter releaser,
Pollution maker.

**Craig Doctor (11)**
**Kingswood Primary School, Corby**

## Litter

Wrapper dropper
Food waster
Gum spitter
Litterbug
Paper flinger
Wall destroyer
Dog messer
Mess maker
Graffiti drawer
Planet destroyer.

**Joshua Jarman (11)**
**Kingswood Primary School, Corby**


## Extinction

Tiger killer
Animal hater
Blood shedder
Death maker
Life destroyer.

**Dante Sharples (9)**
**Kingswood Primary School, Corby**


## War - Haiku

Planet destroyer
Making everyone homeless
Everyone suffers.

**Dominic Devlin (11)**
**Kingswood Primary School, Corby**

## Being Homeless

Being homeless is very bad
Being homeless is very sad
If you're homeless you'll be poor
You'll be the one not answering the door.

If you're homeless you'll have no friends
It's best that you hurry, you're homeless and near the end
If you're homeless you'll end up crying
You'd better be careful, you'll end up dying.

As long as you're homeless, you're a prisoner
You cannot escape, nobody will be there
To save you from a nightmare
When you are homeless you'll sleep in the dirt
If you sleep in the dirt you'll end up hurt.

If you're homeless, you'll get called names
You'll end up depressed and have no mates
If you're homeless you'll be as cold as ice
Without a blanket and bitten by mice.

**Damla Akgul (10)**
**Kingswood Primary School, Corby**


## Being Homeless

Being homeless you end up crying,
This is causing people to stop trying.
Kids afraid and abandoned,
Scared, sad and frightened.

Being homeless you will end up hungry,
Beg for food and have a sore tummy.
Only there's no one to care,
Loneliness, unable to bear.

Being homeless, you're near the end,
No cuddles or any friends,
When you're homeless there's no smiling,
Because sooner or later you will end up dying.

**Lauren Stedman (10)**
**Kingswood Primary School, Corby**

## Rainforest

R ain rattling like a rattlesnake
A ngry at the rainforest being destroyed
I magine the beautiful clear water of the blue waterfall gushing down to the ground
N ice, lovely flowers opening up brightly
F rogs jumping on lily pads and into the pond
O wls building nests in the trees of the rainforest
R ainbows shining over the forest like a light
E xtinct animals dying, not many left
S unshine shining brightly as a camera flashes
T rees like butterflies' wings, swaying like grass.
My lovely rainforest.

**Safanah Riaz (11)**
Linden Primary School, Evington


## Save Her

The ozone layer is getting destroyed,
The Earth is getting very annoyed.

The world is getting warm,
This also causes storms.

The world is being repaired by wizards,
But instead they're getting blizzards.

The Earth is in danger,
People, let's save her.

**Gurdit Singh Dosanjh (10)**
Linden Primary School, Evington

## Pollution

P eople
O ver-use cars
L itter as well
L ife is probably over
U should try to help
T ry to stop using cars
I nstead use your feet
O h please stop polluting
N ow think about the future.

**Ndumiso Nyoni (10)**
Linden Primary School, Evington


## Rainforest

Nothing is stirring
Something strange is occurring
There isn't a sound
Then *crash!*
A tree falls to the ground
A whirlwind of dust
No longer fresh and lush
Habitats destroyed
Animals annoyed.

**Molly Furnival-Phillips (11)**
Linden Primary School, Evington


## War Is . . .

War is danger
War is a cloud of unhappiness
War is women crying
War is destruction of people's homes
War is evil
War, war, make it no more.

**Jaisel Odedra (11)**
Linden Primary School, Evington

## Homeless

H omeless families
O nly drinking dirty water
M oving from street to street
E ating rubbish from bins
L ooking out for each other
E very day they are begging for money
S o be grateful for what you have got
S olemnly say thank you to God.

**Zainab Ahmad (11)**
Linden Primary School, Evington


## Help

H omeless people
O nly drinking dirty water
M any people are dying
E at again and again
L ooking out for people
E agerly need your help
S lowly dying
S ave us, please!

**Nasreen Bhana (10)**
Linden Primary School, Evington


## Pollution

Spreading quicker,
Getting faster,
Climate changer,
Animal killer,
Winter stopper,
Summer loser,
Ozone thinner,
World in danger.

**Karan Chundavadara (11)**
Linden Primary School, Evington

## Litter

L itter is disgusting
I t's ruining our Earth
T he Earth is precious
T ime is running out
E arth is beautiful
R ight now our planet is suffering!

**Eleanor Forté (11)**
Linden Primary School, Evington


## Stop War

S uffering people
T rying to live
O ur children given guns
P laygrounds are gone

W orld crying
A eroplanes flying
R acing towards death.

**Vishnu Godhania (11)**
Linden Primary School, Evington


## Snow

Snowballs falling from the sky.
Children playing and calling.
People chatting and talking.
It is so cold.

**Ella Mowbray, Owen Gamble & Daisy Marsh (9)**
North Leverton Primary School, North Leverton

## Our World Needs To Be A Better Place

Pick up the litter,
Recycle more,
Being homeless is no more.
The rainforest and animals
Are dying of disease
Because of the pollution and poverty.
Racism and war is no more,
Because of the Big Green Poetry Machine.
Our world needs to be a better place.

**Katrina Hayes (10)**
**North Leverton Primary School, North Leverton**


## Go Green!

Go green
Don't be mean
We can all be keen
To keep the world green

Put your litter in the bins
Recycle your tins
Cardboard and paper too
If you don't, the only person you can blame is you

Go green
Don't be mean
We can all be keen
To keep the world green.

**Bethany Bartram (10)**
**North Leverton Primary School, North Leverton**

# Climate Change

C limate change, people in danger,
L ightning storms.
I watch TV, but they're all strangers.
M ost people die is what they say
A nd we watch this day after day.
T ornadoes blow, tsunamis destroy,
E arthquakes rumble.

C oldest conditions for the season
H ottest temperatures
A t the wrong time of year for no reason
N ow we have to
G et ready to save the
E arth.

**Ryan Wilcock (11)**
**Robert Miles Junior School, Bingham**


# It Says

Once there was a poem!
A poem about recycling.
It talked about waste,
It talked about waste, far too much waste;
Metal cans, lights left on, cans, paper.

It talked about how to save the world.
We said, 'How?'
It said, 'Now?'
We said, 'Yes.'
It said, 'Recycle.'
We said, 'Yes.'
It said, 'Reuse.'
We said, 'Yes, sure!'

**Dexter Turnbull (11)**
**Robert Miles Junior School, Bingham**

## Pollution

Why do you drive your cars,
When the distance isn't very far?

Plastic, metal, paper! Why is it not reused?
Our natural resources we will lose!

Why damage the Earth?
Think first about what it is worth.

Help the Earth by saving power,
Don't have a bath, take a shower!

The Earth is precious and strong,
To destroy it would be wrong!

**Dale Thomas (11)**
**Robert Miles Junior School, Bingham**


## Pollution

Why do we waste energy,
Even if it's for a short time?

The factories pollute the air with carbon dioxide.
Why are we doing this?

Why drive cars when the distance isn't far?
Exhaust fumes fill the air.

Why do we do all this?
Why don't we think?
This is causing pollution.
Help save the Earth.

**Lewis Cheung (11)**
**Robert Miles Junior School, Bingham**

## Listen To What We're Doing, The Bad Things

Here's the warning,
Who can stop it?
Global warming,
Only us.

Do your bit,
Don't put rubbish
In a pit.
Use green, grey and blue.

What are they?
I hear you ask.
Wheelie bins, ring a bell?

Don't cut down trees,
Animals call that home!
Please, pretty please!
How would you feel if your home was destroyed?

And as well,
The trees,
We need,
To breathe.

Don't make
Our carbon footprint
Any bigger.

Walk to school,
Or take the bus!
Do whatever will help us!

Do you want
To have a life,
A long, happy life?

Well, the Earth
Won't be here
In a few years,
The way we're going!

So like I said,
Do your bit,
Don't be lazy and mean
Because although it might not seem,
But you've really got to believe . . .

*That*
*We*
*Need*
*To*
*Save*
*Our*
*Earth!*

Please . . .

Who else can?
Only every person in the world,
If they do their bit!

Beauty comes from within,
Let's find it in our Earth!

**Eleanor Cooke (10)**
**Robert Miles Junior School, Bingham**

# Black Mist

All the darkness swirling round,
Murdering without a sound.

Cutting through the cool, clean air,
Get the darkness out your hair.

We need help to stop, please be sane,
The creeping gas gets in your brain.

The black mist will pollute us too,
Help the world, me and you!

The $CO_2$ can come from a bus,
Come on now, help without a fuss.

Television, cars, anything electric,
We need to turn them off, be quick.

This carbon dioxide will be our terrible fate,
Come on, hurry, you just can't wait.

Quick, it's coming here,
It's burning up the atmosphere.

You just turn off any light,
We need to stand and fight.

If anything is not in use,
Turn it off, stop $CO_2$.

And of course you have to walk,
Spread the word, you need to talk.

Your cars produce a nasty gas,
This is your time, don't let it pass.

Help us save the whole wide world,
One person makes a big, big difference.

Now it's time to do your bit,
Please help and stop the big black mist!

**Megan Wills (11)**
**Robert Miles Junior School, Bingham**

## Climate Change Issue

Climate change is a serious issue,
A problem around the world.
Our air is polluted,
Our streets full of litter.
The Poles are melting,
Floods will happen.
It's bad for animals.
Climate change is a serious issue,
A problem which can be solved.
Try walking rather than using your car,
Go on a bus, it's a better kind of transport.
It creates less pollution
Than all the other people in cars.

Do your bit!
Make a difference!
Make our world good.

**Stefan Rose (11)**
**Robert Miles Junior School, Bingham**

## Recycling Madness

Please recycle, lots and lots,
Don't forget those yoghurt pots.
Recycle drink bottles too,
Please don't flush them down the loo.
Also recycle tins,
Don't put them in normal bins.

Please recycle card,
Come on, it's not really that hard.
Don't dump paper in the grey bin,
Recycle it - don't be a sin.
Kitchen rolls too
And the ones from the loo.
Also recycle wood,
I bet you never knew you could.

I hope this is making sense to you,
But listen, still I'm not yet through,
'Cause there's loads of others too,
That's why we need you!

Come on people, you may think I'm mad,
But seriously, the world will go bad,
Unless we recycle lots and lots,
Not just paper and pots.

Our world is running out of space,
Come on, recycle, just in case.
You ask why? Why do we?
Well, don't you see?
They have been planting rubbish underground,
They have been planting rubbish round and round.

When we recycle, we can reuse,
So our natural resources we will not lose.
But now there's no more space,
So come on, recycle, just in case!

**Grace Watts (10)**
Robert Miles Junior School, Bingham

## The Beach

In my mind
I picture the beach
Golden sands, clear indigo water
Waves crashing like crystals
On an expanse of grains . . .

But I am not in the magical place
I fantasise about

I am here amongst an array of rubbish
Peppered on my beautiful beach

The clear indigo water is a mixture
Of murky blue liquid and polluted froth

The crystal waves are nothing like I imagined
They are a crashing roar that sends a dark chill
Down my spine

Why is it like this?
What happened here?

Pollution happened

Pollution ruined my beautiful beach
It came and unbalanced the beauty of nature
And turned it as sour as lemons

We can all make a difference to our world
And save our beautiful beaches
Before it's too late.

*Do your bit!*

**Ellie Clark (11)**
**Robert Miles Junior School, Bingham**

# Climate Change

Some people ignore the signs of climate change,
They think she is just coming and going,
But soon . . .
She is coming to stay.

What can we do?
What can we do
Before everything around us perishes?

Tell us,
Tell us, please!

OK then, but before I begin,
I will tell you,
There are three steps and probably more
Which can help to stop *her!*

Well, to help the animals that are becoming extinct,
Don't ruin their homes,
Don't ruin their lives,
And if you do that you will then know
Your first step towards stopping *her!*

Well, to stop the pollution,
The main cause of *her*,
Don't waste the electricity in your home,
Don't drive around unless you have to
And if you do that, you will then know,
Your second step towards stopping *her!*

Well, to help the environment from all the rubbish,
Don't drop litter, put it in the bin,
Don't waste rubbish, recycle it
And if you do that, you will then know,
Your third step towards stopping *her!*

So if you do all that,
Then you can surely stop *her*
And the melting of the ice and snow,

But . . .

Beware, for she still may come back
And that would be a . . .

*Disaster!*

**Elizabeth Ryder (11)**
Robert Miles Junior School, Bingham

# Litterbugs

When you drop
Some litter
You're destroying
Not just yours, but
*Our*
World!

So listen . . .

Help the world.
When *you* see some litter,
Don't leave it for someone else
To put in the bin!
Do it yourself.
Don't be lazy and mean
To our environment!
Recycling it's called -
Does it ring a bell?

Trust me, it will work.

So sweep the streets,
Nice and clean,
Until they gleam
And then, not just
*You,*
But *everybody* else will have
A better world.

So *please* do your bit!

**Matthew Coughtrey (11)**
Robert Miles Junior School, Bingham

## Stop Bullying

S cared and lonely
T ears soaking my pillow
O ften hurting
P lease let this pain go away

B adly bullied
U nhappy
L onely and frightened
L onely and unhappy
Y ou hurt me really bad
I hate being bullied by people
N ever gonna get unhappy
G oing home, sitting in my bedroom.

**Sineh McFarlane (8)**
**Robin Hood Primary School, Mansfield**


## Stop Bullying

S ad and scared
T ears soaking my pillow
O ften alone
P ainful words

B ruised and hurt
U nhappy thoughts
L onely and sad
L onging for love
Y ou surround me with meanness
I n need of a friend
N ever going to stop
G oing to survive, I will.

**Alex Morey (8)**
**Robin Hood Primary School, Mansfield**

## Stop Bullying

S cared and frightened
T ears my heart out
O ften been hurt
P unched and kicked

B ruised every day
U nhappy and battered
L onely and afraid
L osing friends
Y ou are breaking my heart
I feel like I'm going to cry
N obody loves me
G oing to get bullied forever.

**Owen Ives (8)**
Robin Hood Primary School, Mansfield


## Stop Bullying

S ick and frightened
T ired and alone
O uch, you've hurt me again
P lease leave me alone

B rave but bruised
U pset and tearful
L onely
L ooking for friends
Y ou hate me
I nsecure and scared
N ever feel loved
G oing on and on and on.

**Ryan Southall (8)**
Robin Hood Primary School, Mansfield

## Please Bully

Please bully, stop calling me names
Please bully, don't chase me
Please bully, don't take my dinner money
Please bully, don't push me over
Please bully, don't pull my hair
Please bully, don't spoil my game
Please bully, don't hurt me anymore
Please bully, don't throw me on the floor
Please bully, don't put me up on the fence
Please bully, don't kick me
Please bully, don't punch me
Please bully, don't put your hard mates on me.

**Savannah Southway (8)**
**Robin Hood Primary School, Mansfield**


## Stop Bullying

S ick
T ired
O uch
P roud

B ullied and bruised
U nhappy
L onely
L onging
Y ou hate me
I nside hurting
N ever stopping
G iving up.

**Ryan Caudwell (8)**
**Robin Hood Primary School, Mansfield**

## Please Bully

Please bully, don't call me names.
Please bully, don't punch me.
Please bully, don't kick me.
Please bully, don't bully me.

**Corey Roberts (8)**
Robin Hood Primary School, Mansfield Please bully,


## Bullying

B ig bully
U gly yob
L ying devil
L ittle devil
I gnorant, painful
E vil bully
D evastated.

**Luke West (9)**
Robin Hood Primary School, Mansfield


## Gunshots

G as so poisonous will kill us all
U nbelievable cross of honour
N othing like this I have ever seen
S hots like Christmas lights only with people dropping
H ot bullets flying out of AK47s hitting our men
O thers are dead
T in bullets are everywhere and thick barbed wire like splinters
S trong people with tears down their faces and death on every corner.

**Sam James-Molloy & Henry (11)**
Rockingham Primary School, Corby

# Please Save The Rainforest

Please reader, read this,
Or else you'll face the worst.

Please save the rainforest,
The trees are going down,
Which makes everybody, everybody frown.
Please, please, please save the rainforest,
Every animal will be extinct.

Please save the rainforest,
There will be hardly any fresh air.
Just remember the animals, it won't be fair.
Please, please, please save the rainforest,
Every animal will die.

Please save the rainforest,
Just recycle paper, plastic, or even your bike.
Please reader, do what I have told you.
Please, please, please save the rainforest,
Every animal will be extinct.

Please save the rainforest,
I'm giving you my last warning.
Just stop and think what you can do.
Please, please, pretty please, just save the rainforest,
Every animal will live.

**Meghan Hill (10)**
**Rockingham Primary School, Corby**

## Pollution

Acid rain giving trees pain
Like hurricanes and tornados.
The sewage goes into the seas
And it can cause disease.

The earthquakes cause destruction,
Now the towns need reconstruction.
The polar ice caps are going to melt,
Polluted air is what you have smelt.

Now there are limited animals,
They will think humans are cannibals.
This is what you have done,
Now the Earth is as hot as the sun.

**Sad Maudarbux (11)**
**Rockingham Primary School, Corby**


## The Environment

People kill trees
But we are desperate to breathe.
Does anyone care?
People are dropping litter
And it is bitter.
Does anyone care?
Animals are being hurt
Because of all the horrible dirt.
Does anyone care?
There's pollution in the air
And we should care!

**Latasha Fitzpatrick (11)**
**Ruskin Junior School, Wellingborough**

## Our Environment

Our environment needs to be a better place,
Because it is a great disgrace.
People drop their plastic bottles or maybe a can,
It is disgusting and needs to be banned.
The councils chop trees,
But we need to breathe.

Disgraceful people drop glass on the floor,
You wouldn't like it when it's near your door.
Careless people drop gum on the streets,
And smoking is a habit we need to beat.
Can the pavements take any more?

**Tiffany Wallace (11)**
**Ruskin Junior School, Wellingborough**

## War And Bullying Are Bad - Haikus

Bullying is bad
Children are left being sad
Educate them now.

War and bullies mixed
They are very sick to me
Stop bullying now.

Bullying is bad
It makes you feel very sad
Bullying is bad.

**Hanna Baldwin (11)**
**Ruskin Junior School, Wellingborough**

## Starvation

People are dying,
Why have children got no food?
We should help the poor.

Food is all around,
Why are poor people dying?

Don't waste precious food,
Make sure you eat all your food.
Help the poor right now!

**Stefan Benn (10)**
Ruskin Junior School, Wellingborough

## Violence! - Haikus

Drinking and driving
Can cause people to get hurt
Ban alcohol now!

Suffering people
Innocent people can die
Stop the madness now.

Put guns away now!
Please don't sell any more guns
Put guns away now.

**Richard Simmons (11)**
Ruskin Junior School, Wellingborough

## Stop The War! - Haikus

Alarms bellowing,
Take cover, people cry out,
Stop the war right now!

Bombs are exploding!
Bullets flying through the air,
Stop the war right now!

Stop the dreaded war!
Children looking for shrapnel,
Stop the war right now!

**Bradley Souster (11)**
Ruskin Junior School, Wellingborough


## War Is Bad

W eapons used to survive
A ll people need armour to survive
R unning from the bombs

V ery little children crying
I nnocent people harmed
O ut of your mind
L ooking for danger
E nemies run
N obody is safe
C anon fire heard in the distance
E verybody has a voice.

**Billy Vidler (11)**
Ruskin Junior School, Wellingborough

## Stop The War!

W ill the fighting ever end?
A nother day, another fight
R un from the bombs

V ery sad children cry
I nnocent people die!
O fficers shouting orders
L ots of guns
E xtra police needed
N obody is safe
C aring people helping
E veryone feels scared.

**Kieran Potticary (11)**
Ruskin Junior School, Wellingborough

## War Is Bad - Haikus

Bombs are exploding,
Children dying, mums crying,
We need to help now!

Soldiers dying, *bang!*
Bombs are screeching as they drop,
Children miss their dads.

Stop the war right now!
People falling on the floor,
We need to help now!

**Alfie Parr (11)**
Ruskin Junior School, Wellingborough

## Stop The War, Please - Haikus

Soldiers spy at night,
Anger causes lots of fights!
I hope it's alright.

Stop the violence now!
We need to stop this, but how?
All we do is row!

Children on curfew,
You're inside, they can't hurt you,
Could your dream come true?

Stop the war now, please!
It's like a huddle of bees,
Stop the war now, please.

**Montell Ashby (11)**
**Ruskin Junior School, Wellingborough**


## War - Haikus

Soldiers risking lives,
Children losing their freedom,
Anger all around.

Soldiers suffering,
Guns, bombs, shooting and booming,
People are dying.

Buildings being bombed,
New soldiers shipped in to kill,
Bullets flying low.

**Billy Jones (11)**
**Ruskin Junior School, Wellingborough**

## Pollution - Haikus

Help us save the world.
Decrease the world's pollution.
Help us save the world!

Pollution is bad.
The air is turning dirty.
Pollution is bad!

Ban cars, get walking.
Stop the pollution killing.
Ban cars, get walking!

Get this in your head.
Help the world's ozone layer.
Get this in your head!

**Jason Holt (11)**
Ruskin Junior School, Wellingborough

## Haiku Poem

Beware, war is here!
Move out of your old houses
Or lose your good life.

Watch out for the bombs.
Look out, the bombs are falling.
Shelters protecting.

**Brandon Richards (10)**
Ruskin Junior School, Wellingborough

## No One Cares

Animals dying
The world is crying
But no one cares

Sprayed graffiti
Spied the needy
But no one cares

Chewing gum
Stuck all day long
But no one cares

Bottles and cans
Helpless hands
But no one cares

Cigarette stubs
Burning away
But no one cares.

**Alexa Brannan (11)**
**Ruskin Junior School, Wellingborough**


## Starvation

Why do people die?
People die from starvation
When food is wasted.

More children are dying,
So please do not waste food.
Help the children now.

**Kieran Reeve (10)**
**Ruskin Junior School, Wellingborough**

## Nobody Cares

Polluted lakes,
For goodness sakes,
But nobody cares.

The animals are being killed,
Because we love to build,
But nobody cares.

The ozone layer is crumbling,
Houses are tumbling,
But nobody cares.

There's lots of pollution,
There's an easy solution,
But nobody cares.

**Cain Clarke (11)**
Ruskin Junior School, Wellingborough


## No One Cares

Sweep the street
Or lots of litter you will meet.
But no one cares.

Pavements look like dirty stew
Because of dog poo.
But no one cares.

Glass on the street,
Cutting children's feet.
But no one cares.

**Barrington Abel (10)**
Ruskin Junior School, Wellingborough

# The End Of Days

Polar bears say their prayers
But nobody cares.

Animals are getting killed as we start to build
But nobody cares.

Trees are sliced by a saw to let us draw
But nobody cares.

There's an easy solution but still there's pollution
But nobody cares.

The green environment is turning into a mean environment
Does anybody care?

**Daniel McCullagh (11)**
**Ruskin Junior School, Wellingborough**


# Litter

Litter is nasty, so why do you drop it?
Because we all hate it, why don't you stop it?
Can't you see what you're doing?
We all hate the nappies dropped on the roads.
Can't you see they stink loads?
We hate the chewing gum, the way it gets stuck,
Can't you see, it gets in the muck.
Save the planet, it's in your hands,
I can't see why you don't understand.

**Keeley Dargue (11)**
**Ruskin Junior School, Wellingborough**

## You Cannot Live Without Your Health

H elp hospitals, give them support
E at a balanced diet, eat fruit, veg and meat
A lcohol is horrid, it can be beat
L ess fatty foods could improve our health
T he planet should remember, health is better than wealth
H ealth is important, don't let it go
   Improve your health, let everyone know.

**John Rowlatt (11)**
Ruskin Junior School, Wellingborough


## Cleaner Environment - Haiku

Litter on the floor,
Plastic, sticky gum has made
Us extremely glum.

**Scott Millen Poole (11)**
Ruskin Junior School, Wellingborough


## Litter

Quick, quick,
Pick, pick.

The litter's a crime,
So listen to the rhyme.

Animals dying,
Children crying.

The world's a wreck,
There is a sinking deck.

Help the world,
Before it gets curled.

**Aaron Strong (11)**
Ruskin Junior School, Wellingborough

## Endangered Animals

Animals getting hurt,
Shot, slaughtered, injected,
You can help, please.

Dodos, dragonflies,
Polar bears, say your prayers now,
Please can you help?

Battery hens, why?
Lifetime of captivity,
Think of animals *now!*

**Ryan Betts (11)**
**Ruskin Junior School, Wellingborough**


## Hibernation

When it is winter
Chipmunks and squirrels
Go in their home
With their nuts and food.
While bats hibernate
They sleep upside down.
Animals need food to hibernate.
Help the animals to hibernate.
Animals *need* to live.

**Jodie Wallace (9)**
**St Mary's CE Primary School, Kettering**


## The World Around Us

Save the world by picking up litter.
It saves the animals and the world.
It stops the animals dying
And people choking from it all.
Save the plants and the air
So we can breathe and not cough.

**Katrina Newlyn (9)**
**St Mary's CE Primary School, Kettering**

## Please Don't Cut Down Trees

Please don't cut down trees,
It'll kill animals such as bees.
Also the lovely, lovely owls
Who think their trees are towels.

Leopards use them like settees
And their pillows are the leaves.
Giraffes like the tasty bamboo
Which people are flushing down the loo.

Trees are for animals too,
Not just for me and you.
If you carry on chopping down trees,
You'll be attacked by the stinging bees!

**Grace Sensier (9)**
**St Mary's CE Primary School, Kettering**


## Litter Planet

Polluting our planet
Destroying the animals' habitats
They are dying because of us
Stop litter now!
Animals are becoming extinct
We need to stop it now
It looks horrible
So use the bin
Instead of the planet.
We need animals
So stop it now
Because it looks horrible.
Don't chuck litter in the lake
Because fish live there
Or in the bush
Because it looks horrible
So stop it now.

**Jemma Hughes (8)**
**St Mary's CE Primary School, Kettering**

## Care For Animals

A is for animals, think about their feelings
N is for nature, nature is important, it's what it's all about
I is for imagine, imagine what it would be like without these wonderful animals
M is for make them feel safe, make them feel that they are safe and protected their whole lives
A is for animals, care for them, keep them safe, protect them
L is for love, they need love. Love is the most important thing of all
S is for safety and support, that is what they're waiting for.

**Patricia Anne V Mallare (8)**
St Mary's CE Primary School, Kettering


## A Poem About Our Planet And Litter

Litter is everywhere,
On mountains
And in rivers.
Animals die because of litter,
Litter is bitter.
People get stressed out,
It makes our planet a bad place.
So put the litter in the bin,
Use the bin, that's what they are for.
Get rid of the rubbish!

**Hannah Strickland (9)**
St Mary's CE Primary School, Kettering

## Animals Are Dying

Animals are dying,
All around the world,
Animals like birds and bees,
All live in the trees.

They're beginning to be homeless,
Their homes are being destroyed,
It doesn't help at all,
Life for them is getting harder.

They're trying to survive, but are disappearing,
On the brink of extinction,
Try to save them,
However you can, *now!*

**Yasmin Boyall (9)**
**St Mary's CE Primary School, Kettering**


## Litter Rap

Litter everywhere
At the park
On the streets
There are bins everywhere
Litter is bitter.

Stop dropping it
On the floor
Or anywhere
Litter is bitter.

Remember, put it in the bin
And drop it in
And everyone will be happy
Litter is bitter.

**Jade Leeson (9)**
**St Mary's CE Primary School, Kettering**

## Save The Rainforest

Stop destroying the rainforest,
Where will the monkeys live?
Consider all the animals,
Such as birds, lizards and primates.
Imagine how they feel,
Blue, panicked and hungry,
Longing for a meal.
Trees give us oxygen
And every tree breathes.
All assorted animals will die, that's a pity.
A tree is like a person,
Destroy it and it dies.
For our chopping chainsaws are weapons,
But will we survive?
If we had a mind,
We most definitely would.
Stop cutting down rainforests.
Will any of us survive?

**Lauson Kenyon (9)**
St Mary's CE Primary School, Kettering


## Litter

L itter should stop now
I t is killing wildlife
T oday you can stop it
T oday you can
E veryone needs to help
R ubbish doesn't belong on the floor.
   *Stop it now!*

**Alisha Taylor (9)**
St Mary's CE Primary School, Kettering

## Help The Wolves

Help the wolves, keep them safe!
In a hut or under a tree,
Give some spare change for them.
Help wolves, they are starved,
Give them money.
They need food to keep them alive and strong.
Help the wolves, they are thirsty,
They need water to stay alive
And not die early.
Thank you all for listening,
I hope you do what I said.
Now save their lives, just a penny or two.
Help the wolves.

**Tabitha Catlin (9)**
**St Mary's CE Primary School, Kettering**


## Mill Road Park

The swing is like a rusty car.
The grass is like mud.
The stones are as sharp as spikes.
There was a slide but it got knocked down
Because it had graffiti on it.
The gates are the worst,
They got knocked down as well.
Play around
Run, kick footballs.

**Luca Benedickter (9)**
**St Mary's CE Primary School, Kettering**

## Vegetarians

Animals aren't put on this planet to be eaten,
So be a vegetarian, give animals a life.
Animals give joy to us, let them go free.
Why kill them to eat them?
We have other lovely food, like fruit and veg.
Soon there will be no animals.
Animals have feelings and hearts.
Animals cry.

**Jai Sharma (9)**
**St Mary's CE Primary School, Kettering**

## Love The Planet

Rubbish, rubbish we throw it away,
But we should recycle every day.
From cardboard, paper, plastic and glass,
We should never let the opportunity pass.

Peace man, peace man, be cool, be cool,
Always recycle, don't be a fool.
Save your electricity, your food and your heat,
It's not easy, it's no mean feat.

We've got to love the planet no matter what,
It's the only one we've got.
So save the rainforest, save on water,
We want the planet to live longer *not* shorter.

**Beth Green (8)**
**St Michael's CE Primary School, Lincoln**

## Global Problem, Single Solutions

Help save the planet,
By recycling and reusing.
Make the right decision,
It's the wildlife we're losing.

The trees are being cut down
And the Earth is warming up.
Get around in different ways,
Don't take the car to town.

Switch lights off when you leave the room,
Put your garden waste on the compost.
It's up to us to put things right,
So it will not end in doom.

**Joshua Berry (9)**
St Michael's CE Primary School, Lincoln


## Eco-Friendly

To be eco-friendly you'd best do as I say,
Make it a habit that you do every day.
Recycle paper, glass and cans,
Make sure you minimise your use of vans.
Switch off the light, especially at night,
Use water butts to collect the rain,
Being eco-friendly does not have to be a pain.

**Ellie Redfern (9)**
St Michael's CE Primary School, Lincoln

## Eco Groove

Hey dude, get in the eco groove.
You need to recycle,
You can recycle paper, tins and more . . .
Just knock on a door and say, *'Recycle!'*

Hey dude, get in the eco groove.
You need to turn off things,
Turn off taps, TVs and more . . .
It should be against the law!

Hey dude, get in the eco groove.
Don't have electronic games
Like PSP, PS2 and more . . .
Go outside and explore!

Hey dude, get in the eco groove.
*Eco groove, yeah!*

**Jack Whittam (8)**
**St Michael's CE Primary School, Lincoln**


## Save The World

Turn the tap off when you brush,
Do you really need to flush?
The standby button should not be on,
You're wasting power, that has to be wrong!
You're buying food then not using it,
In our world we're losing it!
You're wasting water
You're wasting food
You're wasting power
*No, no good!*

**Grace Warren**
**St Michael's CE Primary School, Lincoln**

## Planet In Danger

Save our planet
It's where we live
Stop keep taking
It's time to give

Let's take it in our stride
Leave the car, let's walk not ride

Plastic bags, we use too many
Take our own and gain a penny

The sun is getting hotter
The sea is warming up
No good for sea creatures, big or small
Act now before we lose them all

The ice is melting but who lives there?
Some penguins and a big white bear
Where will they go? What will they do?
I don't know, do you?

**Ella Good (8)**
**St Michael's CE Primary School, Lincoln**


## Birds

B e aware of our friends in the sky
I t is too soon to say goodbye
R ead my poem and understand the eco warning
D on't and you will be sad in the morning
S ave them so they can fly!

**Sophie Hill (8)**
**St Michael's CE Primary School, Lincoln**

## I Need To Tell You Something

Chorus:
Come over here, I need to tell you something
About our world
About our world
About our world . . .
It's dying.
We need to tidy the mess we make
Help clean it up
Clean it up
Clean it up . . .
Keep trying.

Reduce litter, it makes it better
Instead of polluting the world
Let's start walking, not just talking
Instead of polluting the world.

Make use of your day, you can still play
Instead of polluting the world
Save the trees, the birds and the bees
Instead of polluting the world.

Use the right bin, don't get in a spin
Stop polluting the world
Turn off the light, enjoy the night
Stop polluting the world.

**Miss Reid's Class**
St Michael's CE Primary School, Lincoln

## Save Our Earth!

Don't cut trees down,
Don't throw junk,
Recycle your paper
And bottles you've drunk!

Switch your lights off,
Turn off your taps,
Recycle cans
And plastic caps.

Put old food in your compost bin
And let it rot away!
Don't let it go to the landfill site,
Recycle it today!

Clear away rubbish,
So animals can play,
If you leave litter it harms them,
Listen to what I say!

Cycle on your way to school
And walk everywhere!
Leave cars at home
And stop pollution in the air!

Obey these eco rules,
Because it is worth
A tiny bit of hard work,
To *save our Earth!*

**Jessica Thursby (8)**
**St Michael's CE Primary School, Lincoln**

## Eco Poem

Recycle, recycle, get out of that car and use a bicycle.
Homeward bound,
Car shares must be found.
Homeward bound car shares,
Come on, save on transport fares.
Don't be cruel, stop on the fuel - environment!
Past the trees, let's stop using all these trees,
For we're wasting paper, please!
Into the garden, use rainwater,
Get out your container.
Ban the hoses,
Save water for your roses.
Get on your wellies,
For you need to get in with the smellies, compost, save, save, save.
Lose the aerosols for we need to pass
And save the world from all the gas.
Recycle glass, plastic and cardboard too,
Green, brown and black, we must use the right bins through
and through.
Switch off computers, TVs and save the world's energy for our
future children.
Don't delay, do it today!

**Dominic Marshall (8)**
St Michael's CE Primary School, Lincoln


## Paper, Paper

Put the paper in the recycling bin
So it will go *ting, ting, ting.*
Make recycled paper out of old stuff
And make it tough.

**Victoria Aitken (10)**
St Michael's CE Primary School, Lincoln

## Good And Bad

Polluted air, a person is going to care,
Smoke and dust just everywhere.

Polish the trees,
Clean the air for the bees.
The grass grows up to our knees.

The sun shines, leave the coal in the mines,
Bye-bye acid rain, you were such a pain.

Polluted air, polluted air! Go away,
Never come back any other day.

**Henry Hutchings (11)**
**St Michael's CE Primary School, Lincoln**


## The Eco Detective

Who left the light on,
Wasting electricity?
Who left the tap on,
Wasting all the water?
Who left the heating on
And used up all the oil?
Who left their slippers off
And wore their socks out?

Who switched the light off,
Saving electricity?
Who turned the tap off,
Saving all the water?
Who switched the heating off,
Saving all the oil?
Who wore their slippers?
No more worn out socks!

**Nicholas Scott (8)**
**St Michael's CE Primary School, Lincoln**

## My Poem

Eco time is near.
Time for joy and time for cheer.

Want a plane with no fuel.
It's going to be so cool.

It can stop the planet dying
And all the wars and all the hate.
Please eco day don't be late.

E nvironmentally friendly
C ompost bin
O ne less light can make a difference.

**Robert Westwood**
**St Michael's CE Primary School, Lincoln**

## A World In Disgrace

Everywhere is polluted,
There's nothing left.
Rivers, lakes, seas and oceans,
All polluted with people's waste.
Yuck!

Greenhouse gases, $CO_2$,
All killing the ozone.
We must stop polluting the world,
To stop our planet from dying.

**Dominic Contessa (11)**
**St Michael's CE Primary School, Lincoln**

## An Eco-Friendly Poem

E nvironmentally friendly is a great way to be
C o-ordinate our actions and we can make a difference you see
O pportunities are everywhere, try one, then two, then three!

**Jake Hill (11)**
**St Michael's CE Primary School, Lincoln**

## Eco Poem

Switch off lights, TVs and computers,
Because they waste coal and electricity
And we don't have very much coal left!

Bike or walk to school instead of going by car,
Because all the car fumes come out from your car
And this affects global warming.
If you can't go to school without using a car,
Then try to park and stride.

You can do your part by planting plants and trees.
Plants and trees provide oxygen.
Reuse an old shopping bag,
You can do this by taking an old bag shopping.

Don't let taps drip
Because 10 gallons of water
Can power a computer for one hour.

**Alexander Staniforth (9)**
St Michael's CE Primary School, Lincoln


## Recycling

Recycling, recycling,
The best thing to do!
You could even have
A solar panel or two!
You have been warned
About global warming,
Now the storm clouds
Are forming.
You had better start
Helping the Earth,
Before the next generation's birth!
If you don't do it in time,
Don't blame me for your crime!

**Matthew Thompson (10)**
St Michael's CE Primary School, Lincoln

# The Eco Poem

The grass is green, the sky is blue,
Do you want to ruin this too?
It does not take all your day
To put some silly rubbish away.
It would be best to use the green bin,
But it's known to us as the *recycling bin*.

The day is bright, the night is dim,
You really want to ruin this too?
It does not take all your day to flick a switch,
It will change your day.
If you do not need the lights that are on,
Then turn them off, you're doing nothing wrong.
The thing you use is the *light switch*.
There are also other things you can turn off,
Like your TV, computer and other electrical things.

The path is free, the road is not,
So walk to school, but if not,
Share your car with family and friends,
That don't live that far away.
The thing you can do, it's not too hard,
Just *walk to school,* you will soon get that green card.

**Ellie Gibbon (10)**
St Michael's CE Primary School, Lincoln


# Compost

C an you save our planet today
O r will our world fade away?
M y message today is crystal clear
P lease recycle or the end is near
O ver and over we can make old new
S tart today, it's up to you
T his is my message, please help us now,
  ask for information and we can show you how.

**Elloise Long (9)**
St Michael's CE Primary School, Lincoln

## Eco Travel Poem

Go on holiday to the sea,
Eco children do not hurt the environment.
Do we take the car?
Do we take the bike, or do we take the train?
Eco children do not hurt the environment.

Some prefer cars, some prefer bikes,
Some prefer trains that run on electricity.
Some prefer solar-powered buses
Eco children do not hurt the environment.

Planes use fuel, polluting the air,
Vehicle fumes harm people who have asthma.
Making new roads damages the Earth,
Eco children do not hurt the environment.

People wanting many cars harm the environment,
Driving badly wastes fuel.
Too many lorries pollute the air,
Eco children do not hurt the environment.

**Matthew Scott (10)**
**St Michael's CE Primary School, Lincoln**


## My World

E verything matters
N ever say *we can't help it*
V egetation is dying, animals are starving
I ce is melting, slowly shrinking the polar bears' habitat
R ainforests are disappearing
O zone layer is evaporating
N o one seems to care
M an's greed is rising
E veryone can make a difference
N ot tomorrow, *today*
T ime is running out.

**Joseph Brundell (9)**
**St Michael's CE Primary School, Lincoln**

## Eco-Friendly

We need to help the world,
But how can we?
You can recycle your mobile phones.
How can we be more eco-friendly?

We need to help the world,
But how can we?
We can all have water butts in our gardens.
How can we be more eco-friendly?

We need to help the world,
But how can we?
You can have a wind turbine outside your house.
How can we be more eco-friendly?

**Megan Rowland (9)**
**St Michael's CE Primary School, Lincoln**


## Eco Poem

Recycle, recycle,
Please recycle.
Cardboard, paper and glass,
That's all we ask!

Recycle, recycle,
Please recycle,
And help to save our land.

Recycle your paper,
To help save our trees,
That's all we ask.
*Please, please, please.*

**Emily Gatford (9)**
**St Michael's CE Primary School, Lincoln**

## Save Our Planet

S ave water by turning off taps while brushing your teeth
A walk, a run or a cycle whenever you can is better than using
　　　　　　　　　　　　　　　　　　　　　　　　　　the car
V ans and lorries will be reduced on the roads if we recycle what
　　　　　　　　　　　　　　　　　　　　　　　　　　we can
E co-friendly is the way to be

T he trees help us breathe, so we need to save forests
H ave a compost heap in your garden
E lectrical appliances such as TVs should be switched off, not left on standby

P ut up a washing line because the tumble dryers use too
　　　　　　　　　　　　　　　　　　　　　　　　much electric
L et's turn down the heating and put on a jumper
A spidistra plants help pollution, so maybe we should all have one!
N o to pesticides on our vegetables and salads
E nergy efficiency is important for our appliances such as
　　　　　　　　　　　　　　　　　　　　　washing machines
T urn off the lights when you're not in the room!

**Phoebe Erm (8)**
St Michael's CE Primary School, Lincoln


## Eco-Child

I am an eco-child
I want to live in an eco-world
I want to swim in a light blue sea that is free from pollution
I want to walk in a healthy green field with bunnies and birds all
　　　　　　　　　　　　　　　　　　　　　　　　　around me
I want to ride my bike in the fresh, clean air
We must be good to the environment if we want our world to last.

**Sam Perkins (7)**
St Michael's CE Primary School, Lincoln

## Eco-Friendly

E very time you leave a room you should turn off the lights
C lean your car with rainwater, it makes a lovely shine
O nly we can save the planet

F or other people to enjoy
R emember to always recycle your cans
I n the special bins we provide
E ven if you're in a rush
N ever forget to do the above
D o it now before it's too late
L et's work together to make the world great
Y es, we all can be
    *Eco-friendly!*

**Jessica Fenwick (8)**
St Michael's CE Primary School, Lincoln


## Eco-Friendly

*(To the tune of 'He's Got the Whole World in His Hands')*

The whole world needs to be eco-friendly.
There are plants in this world that are green,
There are trees in this world that are green,
Green, green, green, green, green!

We need to be eco, eco-friendly.
We need to be eco, eco-friendly.
We need to be eco, eco-friendly,
Green, green, green, green, green!

We need to look after the birds and bees,
We need to look after the plants and the trees.
So why don't you, ou, ou?
Yeah!

**Amy Hall (8)**
St Michael's CE Primary School, Lincoln

## Eco Dan

This is a poem about Eco Dan
Better known as the recycle man
He always goes to charity shops
To buy his trousers and his tops.

Solar panels are on his roof
And double glazed windows make his home soundproof
His house is powered by wind turbines
And he hangs his washing out on the line.

He never uses a car or bus
But he prefers to walk with us
But he has been known to use a bike
If it is too far to hike.

He likes to use cloth bags to carry his CDs and his mags
He has his own compost bin, all grass and leaves go in
So please take note and be more like Dan
And recycle whenever you can!

**James McKirdy (9)**
St Michael's CE Primary School, Lincoln


## Green Bin

We have a green bin
And put lots of things in.
Cardboard, plastic, paper too,
Bottles, cans cleaned right through.
These are things we need to save,
To keep the planet we must behave.

**Christopher Appleby (10)**
St Michael's CE Primary School, Lincoln

# Help!

They say it's global warming,
Something has to be done.

We need to stop the pollution,
We need to save our planet.

We need to help our wildlife,
As they can't help themselves.

We need to help the plants and trees,
As we need clean air to breathe.

We need to help the children around the world,
They are our future, we need to show them we care.

**Eleanor Burrows (10)**
**St Michael's CE Primary School, Lincoln**


# Eco-Schools

E nvironmentally friendly
C onserve electricity
O rganic products

S elling vegetables
C ollecting old items
H ydro electricity
O pen a recycling bin!
O ceans and seas will benefit
L ess driving
S ave wildlife

**Liam Smalley**
**St Michael's CE Primary School, Lincoln**

## Eco Schools

E verybody to use less paper
C an help to turn the taps off
O il spilling is bad, like driving everywhere

S top wasting electricity by turning the computer off
C an try to help, so can you
H owever you need to be careful not to be disruptive
O nward and forward, don't waste water
O xygen is going because of wasting paper and us wasting trees
L ove the environment.

**Louisa Moxhay-Baker (10)**
St Michael's CE Primary School, Lincoln


## Eco Poem

E nvironmentally friendly is the way to go.
C aring for your world.
O ne shut down computer can save the world.

F ind time to be eco-friendly.
R ecycling anything you find.
I t's time to save the world.
E veryone can do it.
N o excuses.
D on't forget to turn the telly off.
L ights off, we're eco-friendly now.
Y ou can make a difference!

**Lauren Westwood**
St Michael's CE Primary School, Lincoln

## Recycle

R ecycle plastic bottles and cans
E nvironmental damage increasing
C ycle to school and work
Y oung people can help to save the planet
C rushed cans are made new again
L ights can be turned off when not in use
E veryone can do their bit to help.

**Tim Williams (8)**
St Michael's CE Primary School, Lincoln


## Untitled

I am a can of cola on the supermarket shelf,
Along comes a boy one day and drinks me down.
I do hope he puts me in the recycling bin,
So I can come back as a tin of beans.

**William Lupton (8)**
St Michael's CE Primary School, Lincoln


## The Future

Roses are red,
Violets are blue,
If you don't recycle,
They won't be there for you.

**Rebecca Clark (9)**
St Michael's CE Primary School, Lincoln

## Kick Away Climate Change!

Climate change can be rearranged
If we swap our actions
Even a little bit of help
Can break down a lot of factions
Everybody shout it out
Send the message along
Help every bit of the climate change
Then everyone can sing their song
Now it's time for me to go
Please be eco-friendly and let the world flow!

**Saffiah Sanders-Bailey (9)**
St Swithun's CE Primary School, Retford

## Litter

L is for litter
I is for in the bin
T is for take it to a bin
T is for trash
E is for environment which needs to be better
R emember, pick up *litter!*

**Emily Sly (10)**
St Swithun's CE Primary School, Retford

## Litter

L itter, stop dropping it
I ncredible mistake to make
T ell other people to stop
T ell people to bin it
E veryone can change the world
R ecycle what you can.

**Kai Denovan (10)**
St Swithun's CE Primary School, Retford

## The Animal World

A is for animals, all cute and fluffy
N is for nature, so don't spoil it
I is for intelligence and dolphins have it
M is for monkeys, all cheeky and sweet
A is for alligator, all angry and annoyed
L is for leopard creeping very low and very sly
S is for sloth, all slow and steady

A is for animals, some kind, some not
N is for nature, help save it
D is for dolphins who jump the waves

E is for elephants, all big and strong
X is for eXtinction, so help save the animals
T is for turtles that swim in the east Australian current
I is for iguana with its super long tongue
N is for narwhal with its huge long tooth
C is for captivity, where animals are kept
T is for tiger who will creep up on you
I is for in danger, which animals are
O is for option, so make your option to save them
N is for nature, so help save it because good opinions count.

**Jade Swan (10)**
St Swithun's CE Primary School, Retford


## Being Homeless!

Being homeless isn't to be joked about,
Being homeless you will get soaked!
Being homeless you'll be cold all day,
Being homeless with nowhere to stay.

Being homeless you won't have any friends,
Being homeless your bad luck will never end!
Being homeless just isn't fair,
Being homeless . . . *you should care!*

**Jemma Creasy-Woodward (10)**
St Swithun's CE Primary School, Retford

## Save The Rainforest

Save the rainforest,
Save nature,
Save trees and forest life,
Save animals from extinction,
Save their homes.

Make it better for them,
Put an end to it,
Stop cutting down trees
Because we are destroying animals' homes
And they are dying.

**Ashley Mattingley (10)**
**St Swithun's CE Primary School, Retford**


## Save Our World!

If you pick up your litter
your streets will be shinier than glitter.
When people drop trash
an animal's life might crash.
If you pick up litter you will get fitter.
If you drop your clutter, you're a nutter.

**Yumi Li Vi (9)**
**Sneinton CE Primary School, Sneinton**


## Litter - Haikus

Mess is so stinky
Mess is weighing the world down
Put stuff in the bin.

Help the world, please
Litter doesn't help, please stop
I really mean it.

**Sophie Pearce (9)**
**Sneinton CE Primary School, Sneinton**

## Litter

Litter can decay
It can rot and decompose
Then it gets spoilt.

It attracts insects
Other things like mice and rats
And other things too.

Fungus can be bad
Fungus is not very nice
Fungus is smelly.

Litter goes in bins
It can't go on playground floors
It's not hygienic.

**Owen Newton (9)**
Sneinton CE Primary School, Sneinton


## Disgusting Litter

We need to keep clean
We need to put litter in the bin
We need to keep the world clean
If we don't the floor will get messy.
Put litter in the bin because if we don't
And we just keep putting it on the floor
It will make the floor go bitter.

**Leah Collingham (8)**
Sneinton CE Primary School, Sneinton

## Put Litter In The Bin

We have got to put litter in the bin
To make the world a better place to live in.

Put litter in the bin to save our world within.
If you drop litter put it in the bin.

Don't put litter on the floor or you will get poor.
If you put litter on the floor you will get a fine from the law.

**Jade Clarke (9)**
Sneinton CE Primary School, Sneinton


## Litter

Do not put litter on the floor
Don't throw litter or you will get bitter
Litter is rubbish, litter is junk
Litter is smelly, litter stinks
Litter is trash.

**Lavantie Cameron (9)**
Sneinton CE Primary School, Sneinton


## Animals And Extinction

Animals are killed
Because we are
Cutting forests down
And destroying them.

Animals are killed
And their homes are
Destroyed because of
Our buildings.

Animals are killed
And exterminated
Do not kill them.

**Ali Naseer (8)**
Sneinton CE Primary School, Sneinton

## Animals And Extinction - Haikus

Please save animals
Because we are killing them
For our coats and shoes.

Don't kill animals,
We should help them and breed more
So animals live.

Animals need help,
Please help animals to live,
Animals are killed.

So please let them live,
Please do not kill animals,
So let them live, please.

**Ben Flavill (9)**
Sneinton CE Primary School, Sneinton

## Litter - Haikus

Litter can go bad.
Put our litter in the bin.
It attracts insects.

Litter is smelly.
So let's put it in the bin
To help each other.

**Billie Rose (8)**
Sneinton CE Primary School, Sneinton

# Young Writers Information

We hope you have enjoyed reading this book - and that you will continue to enjoy it in the coming years.

If you like reading and writing poetry drop us a line, or give us a call, and we'll send you a free information pack.

Alternatively if you would like to order further copies of this book or any of our other titles, then please give us a call or log onto our website at www.youngwriters.co.uk

**Young Writers Information
Remus House
Coltsfoot Drive
Peterborough
PE2 9JX**

**(01733) 890066**